Toward an
UNDERSTANDING
of
TRANSITIONAL
MINISTRIES

Ross T. Lucas, Ph.D., M.Div.

ISBN: 978-1-105-26751-2

Book interior & cover design by E. McAuley:
www.impluviumstudios.com

Contents

Introduction

FIVE PEOPLE SAT AROUND A TABLE IN SILENCE, silence born out of the resignation of their pastor. It hadn't been a total surprise, but hearing the words, "I'm resigning. Consider this my two-month notice," had been hard to hear.

Bob, the chairman of the church council, who was also the church moderator, finally asked the question that was on everyone's mind, "What do we do now?"

There was no answer.

Finally, Jennifer, the church clerk, said, "I suppose we ought to call the region offices and see what they suggest."

The next morning, Bob made the call. A secretary answered the phone and asked, "What can I do for you?"

Bob responded, "I'm Bob Smithers, moderator of the Everywhere Community Church. Our pastor just resigned and I'd like to talk to the regional executive minister."

"I'm sorry to hear that," the secretary replied. "Please hold while I see if he's available."

After a few long moments, the phone was picked up by the regional exec. He identified himself by name and then continued, "Bob, I'm sorry to hear your pastor resigned. I wasn't aware he was considering leaving your church. How can we help you?"

Bob took a deep breath before answering. "Pastor Phil has been with us for a long time, at least it seems like a long time to me. Last night he announced to the church council that he was going to another church in a different denomination. What are the appropriate steps we need to take?"

There followed a long conversation during which the regional exec gathered information and told Bob that he'd be calling Pastor Phil. He promised to get back to Bob later that day.

The scenario above is repeated many times, with many variations, across the nation and even within smaller denominations and regional areas. What happens next varies from denomination to denomination and from region to region.

First and foremost, most churches in transition will be concerned about how to find someone to fill the pulpit on Sunday morning. It's hard to see everything a pastor does beyond the most public role of preaching. In the back of the mind of many moderators—or whoever represents the church to the region—is the fear that the church will flounder without a person to lead them spiritually. Many people often interpret "leading spiritually" to mean "preaching." The most important thing for a church in transition, whether or not they realize it, is to relieve that first and most pressing anxiety. Other roles the pastor fulfills—like pastoral care, administrative activity, and maintaining connections with other religious functions in the community—may or may not have been considered by the church.

The executive minister will have to handle the above scenario, or something like it, on a regular basis. More than likely, this scenario will repeat several times a year. Sometimes the transition to a new pastor is quite straightforward and runs smoothly, in other instances this can be a period of time where a church is in great turmoil.

In more recent years, the role of the interim pastor has been recognized as a significant influence in a church being able to call a suitable, settled pastor. The region that has an executive who's aware of the importance of the interim pastor is a fortunate region. However, even if denominational leaders are well-educated about the role of the interim, there are other church entities that may not understand the importance of the person going into the interim position.

A long time ago, churches were primarily looking for someone to preach on Sunday and perhaps take care of funerals while they search for a settled pastor. That's changed, or is changing, and even the terminology surrounding these roles is changing. At one time, all we talked about was someone who would be the interim pastor. Now we hear more formal terms, such as "Transitional Pastor" and "Intentional Interim Pastor." Churches need to be able to understand the differences in these roles so a good choice of interim can be made.

When it comes to the person who will serve as the interim pastor, there's still a lack of understanding about what the position is about. Back in the days when all the church wanted was someone to preach on Sunday mornings, almost anyone with preaching experience could do the job. Preaching experience wasn't even a *requirement*. Men and women wanting to go into ministry could use these interim positions as a way of sharpening their preaching skills.

It would be helpful for denominational executives, churches, and individuals who are considering doing interim work to have a better understanding of what it means to hire an Interim Pastor, a Transitional Pastor, or an Intentional Interim Pastor.

My Journey Toward Transitional Ministry

My own journey in ministry started when I felt called to ministry during my senior year of high school in 1963. During my college years at Indiana State University in Terre Haute and then during seminary—a span of about eight years—I was called on to do pulpit supply when a settled pastor had to be away. When I started in my own settled ministries in 1971, I was pastor of small, single-staff-person churches. There weren't even paid secretaries in those churches. I later spent seven years working with two Kiowa Indian churches in Oklahoma. When I returned to Indiana in January of 1981, I was pastor of a church that had me as full-time paid staff working with as many as five additional part-time staff members. In 1990, I came to Michigan and took a position as a pastoral counselor and psychologist.

In 2005, I was transitioning out of psychology and pastoral counseling and my friend Rev. Tucker Gunnerman asked me to take my first interim position. He introduced me to the concept of transitional ministry. For the last fifteen years, I've focused my attention on Transitional, Interim, and Intentional Interim Ministry. It has been an interesting and enlightening fifteen years.

Who This Book Will Benefit

The book is intended to be useful for three distinct groups. First, it will give those who are seeking to *perform* transitional ministry some tools and understanding of what that ministry involves. It's sometimes assumed that being a transitional pastor is the same as being a settled pastor. It isn't. To be sure, tasks may overlap, but the way an interim pastor and a settled pastor orient themselves to these tasks can be quite different. The differences will be clear by the end of the book.

Second, I want this book to help denominational leaders to understand what a Transitional or Intentional Interim Pastor can do for a congregation that's in need of a settled pastor. This will enable them to pave the way for the transitional pastor.

Third, this book may be of help to individual congregations as they seek someone to function as their transitional pastor. In my denomination, there's been little attention paid to what a transitional pastor can offer a church, what a church can expect of a transitional minister, and what the transitional minister may expect of a church in return.

I trust that those who use this guide will find it helpful in performing ministry in varied and sometimes challenging situations.

Chapter 1:
Terminology

THE FIRST THING YOU'LL NEED is an understanding of the terminology I'll be using. Different denominations and congregational settings may use different terminology. What I use here comes from my experience in Baptist settings and supplemental training seminars. If you're from a different background, you may translate these terms to fit your own denomination and setting.

Over the course of the last few decades, there's been a shift in the terminology we use to describe ministry. When someone is identified as a member of the clergy, there are many possible ways to understand what "clergy" means. "Clergy" could refer to a pastor of a local church, a minister of music, a chaplain in the hospital or military, a pastoral counselor, or it might involve some other form of ministry.

The same can be said about the term "ministry" itself. There are those who consider ministry to be the work of the pastor of the church, or the work of a person who ministers to people who are sick or injured, or even the work of a person who minsters to people with mental health issues. From a church perspective, any vocation that involves a calling by God to serve God through service to others could be deemed "ministry." The broadness or narrowness of the definition is a function of the person doing the interpreting. From my personal perspective, there are innumerable ministries.

When I began my own journey into interim ministry, one of my biggest hurdles was understanding the complexity of term "interim ministry." I read books and attended training events. I've even been asked by religious groups outside of my own to lead training events related to Transitional, Interim, and Intentional Interim Ministry. A continuing difficulty has been explaining the difference between these three complex forms of ministry and the more rudimentary task of filling a pulpit until a settled pastor can be called. It's my hope that this book will help others understand some of the differences and, more specifically, what a Transitional, Interim, and Intentional Interim Pastor can each do for a church.

I started out performing a lot of pulpit supply: preaching when a pastor was on vacation or at a conference or some other occasion. At the time, I didn't understand there to be a lot of difference between interim ministry and pulpit supply. In my mind, and I think in the expectations of the churches I served, the job requirements were about the same. I would preach on Sunday and provide minimal pastoral care until the pastor returned or another settled pastor was called to the church.

During my first official interim position, I met the Rev. Paul Pachazka. He had been an Intentional Interim Pastor for some time and made me aware of the difference between an "Interim Pastor," an "Intentional Interim Pastor," and a "Transitional Pastor." The more I delved into interim ministries, the more apparent the distinction became. I will go into further detail about the distinctions between these roles in Chapter 3.

Helpful Terms and Definitions

Terminology facilitates understanding. Your group may use different terminology than I do, and I can't assume everyone will understand what I'm referring to simply because a term seems common to me. Use this section as a reference if you aren't sure what a particular term means. I'll say enough about each term to allow it to be translated by other denominations or groups.

Settled Pastor – This is a term used for someone who's performing ministry with the expectation that they'll be serving a particular church and congregation for the foreseeable future, or for a specified time during which the congregation will not be seeking anyone else to take over.

Call – A decision by a congregation that a specific person should be leading them in some area of ministry. A call can be open-ended or closed-ended. It may be contractual, or it may be a verbal agreement. A call is very similar to the concept of employing someone, but with the understanding that the congregation believes God is directing them to the individual being called.

Open-Ended Call – Some churches call a pastor with the expectation the pastor will be there for the foreseeable future. In these cases, there usually isn't a contract specifying the length of time the person will serve. It's assumed the person's service will continue until either the individual or the congregation comes to believe it's time for a change.

Closed-Ended Call – Some churches call a pastor with the expectation that the pastor will be there only for a specified length of time. There's usually a contract specifying the length of time the person will serve. It's assumed the person's service will end at the specified time and that continued service would require another call and contract.

Clergy – Someone who's involved in an area of ministry approved of by a congregation or denominational group, and who has been singled out for that area of service by the church. In addition, the person will have education and training in preparation for the work they'll be doing

Pulpit Supply – Someone who preaches when a regular pastor is absent from the pulpit, or who fills in when there's no one who can preach regularly. Pulpit supply usually only lasts for a week or two.

Ongoing Pulpit Supply – Pulpit supply which continues over an extended period of time. It may be several months in duration.

Interim Minister (or Pastor) – A minister or person who helps a church keep functioning when a church is between settled pastors.

Transitional Minister (or Pastor) – A minister or person who helps a church keep functioning between settled pastors, but who is also involved in helping the church move forward in the pastoral search process.

Intentional Interim Minister (or Pastor) – A minister or person who helps a church keep functioning between settled pastors, but who is also involved in helping the church move forward in the pastoral search process. An Intentional Interim will have specialized training to help a church understand its identity and goals before calling a settled pastor.

Focus Point – There are Five Focus Points (sometimes referred to as "Developmental Points") which are important for a church to examine before calling a settled pastor. These are: Heritage, Vision/Mission/Identity, Connections, Leadership, and Future.

Interim Ministry Network – A multi-denominational organization that provides training for Intentional Interim Ministers (or Pastors) and maintains a listing of people who are members and who have completed the training.

Full-Time Position – A position where the pastor has the income from church work as their primary income source. Hours vary and are determined by the need for services rather than a specific number of hours.

Part-Time Position – A position where the pastor isn't expected to spend unlimited hours in service to a church. The amount of time is usually contracted with the church. The term has fallen out of popularity because a pastor's work is such that an hourly approach isn't helpful. [See "Bi-Vocational"]

Bi-Vocational Pastor – A position where a person serves a church in some role, but who also has to maintain other sources of income. At one time, bi-vocational was referred to as "part-time."

Senior Pastor – In a multi-staff church, the senior pastor is the head or leader of pastoral functions. In single-staff churches, the single pastor is sometimes referred to as the senior pastor.

Search Committee – Sometimes referred to as the "pulpit committee" or the "pastoral search committee." A group of congregants who've been given the responsibility of screening pastoral candidates and bringing a final recommended individual to the church for consideration.

Pulpit Committee – Sometimes referred to as the "search committee" or the "pastoral search committee." A group of congregants who've been given the responsibility of screening pastoral candidates and bringing a final recommended individual to the church for consideration.

Transition Team – A team of congregants who oversee the church's examination of itself while the church is between settled pastors. The exact duties and the extent of the duties can vary from congregation to congregation.

Church Board (or Church Council) – The governing body of the church. In congregational settings, the congregation as a whole is the governing body and the church council or church board acts on behalf of the congregation in between full business meetings of the church.

Lay Pastor – An individual who's been recognized by the church as having leadership skills. However, the person hasn't completed requirements for formal ordination.

Denomination – A group of churches with similar ideas. Different denominations may be organized in different ways.

Judicatory – An authority in a denominational setting.

Ordination – A formal rite that acknowledges an individual is called by God to serve the church in some way. There are various requirements, including but not limited to: education, meeting with an ordination council, and experience in the area of ministry the individual is being ordained to.

Chapter 2:
Forms of Ministry

MINISTRY TAKES ON MANY DIFFERENT FORMS. Paul names some of the forms—apostles[1], teachers, and evangelists—but there are others. All of these ministries have some aspects in common, but each form has its own unique features. For example, a minster of Christian education (someone responsible for education related to religious faith) will be trained and oriented differently than a minister of music (someone responsible for the way music is used to promote religious faith). Chaplains (military, hospital, police, hospice, etc.) facilitate a person's struggle with life in terms of their religious faith in a setting that isn't primarily religious in nature. Chaplains will have differing perspectives amongst themselves and will also differ from other ministry disciplines.

A local church pastor will have similarities to all of these other forms of ministry and will still have differences that set them apart. Though unrealistic, some people may expect a pastor to be able to perform every different form of ministry with excellence. Indeed, the local pastor may be called upon to function in many different roles. Local pastoral ministry is a generalist occupation that includes teaching, preaching, seeing to the mental wellbeing of congregants, planning and strategizing for a church, evangelism, caring for physical needs of congregants, and responding to emergency situations to reassure people that God is present with them. A pastor

---

1   1 Corinthians 12:28, Ephesians 4:11

may perform all these tasks and more, but it's a mistake to believe any pastor will excel in every area that's considered to be pastoral.

Over the last few decades especially, ministry has become more and more specialized. Consider the hospital chaplain, who must fulfill specific expectations regarding their education and experience: They must be skilled at working with people who are grieving, people who are in the process of dying, and people who are struggling to understand why they're ill, or injured, and what that will mean for their future. In formal settings, chaplains are usually expected to have several units of clinical pastoral education in addition to a basic four-year college degree and a theological degree of some form. Military chaplains are even more specialized. They're also expected to know how to work with people who have religious connections different from their own.

As recently as twenty years ago, it was thought that any pastor could step into being a hospital chaplain. There was once an opening for a hospital chaplain in my area and someone asked me if I'd be interested in applying for the position. When I told them that a hospital chaplain was a specialized field, I wasn't sure they understood. While I was very well trained in my own field of pastoral ministry (pastoral counseling), I didn't have the specialized training to be a hospital chaplain. I wouldn't have been comfortable doing that work without taking on additional clinical pastoral education. Confusion about these requirements persists to this day.

Similar problems come with the role of minister of Christian education. A person looking for a position in a church setting might claim to be a minister of Christian education without any real understanding of what that position demands. It might be that they have a background in general education without any training in how that relates to the church and to the church's mission. To be a minister of Christian education requires an understanding of the process of education at many different age levels, as well as an understanding how that fits into the overall mission of the church.

When I began ministry more than fifty years ago, all pastors were considered, to some extent, to be counselors. It was understood that if a person had education as a pastor (or even if they were called as a pastor without education), they would also be able to offer counseling to individuals and couples. In the minds of some, there was little difference between pastoral counseling and mental health counseling.

As awareness of different fields of counseling grew, so did the realization that pastoral counseling was unique. The pastoral counselor has training in a mental health discipline, as viewed through a theological lens, and they are recognized by their religious body. In addition, the pastoral counselor is trained to integrate the spiritual life of an individual with their particular mental health issues.

Many pastors have come to recognize that, while some counseling is a natural part of pastoral duties, there's a level of expertise that goes beyond what most pastors are competent to perform unless they have training. This level of expertise is more closely associated with mental health counseling, and a detailed study of mental illness is part of their training. At one time, the American Association of Pastoral Counselors (which has since been taken over by Clinical Pastoral Education) required a person to have a minimum of two advanced degrees to be a part of that body. One of the advanced degrees was required to be in pastoral ministry. The other was at least a master's degree in a related mental health field. That was in addition to supervised field experience and at least one unit of clinical pastoral education.

Despite the growing distinction in the field of pastoral counseling, there are pastors who still claim to be able to offer counseling that's basically the equivalent of "mental health counseling with a Christian twist." From this perspective, all mental health issues are interpreted as "spiritual" issues that can be approached by educating people about what the scriptures say. This is sometimes called "Christian counseling" and some practitioners are quite good at what they do. Other persons use the label to justify offering counseling without any real training or in-depth understanding of the relationship between mental health and spiritual health.

Once, a man who wanted to offer counseling in weight management told me that, since he couldn't advertise himself as a "counselor," a legally protected title, he would instead advertise himself as a pastoral counselor specializing in weight control issues. Since there's no legal protection to the label "pastoral counselor," anyone can call themselves a pastoral counselor and no one can object. If objections are raised, those objections are often framed as an attack on freedom of religion. This is still an ongoing issue. While some persons are doing good work under the label of pastoral counselor, others are actively harming the mental health of individuals in their care.

The Interim Pastor or Transitional Pastor is another specialized field that isn't very clearly understood, and suffers from similar misconceptions.

Chapter 3:
Types of Interim Ministry

I BEGAN WORKING IN TRANSITIONAL MINISTRY IN 2005. I was asked to take on a transitional ministry position because of my background and skills in pastoral counseling and psychology. Just prior to this shift in focus, I had served as a pastoral counselor for fifteen years. Prior to that, I had served as a local church pastor for over twenty years. However, I hadn't had any specific training in transitional ministry.

There are at least four forms of ministry lumped together under the "interim" label: Interim Pastor, Transitional Pastor, Intentional Interim Pastor, and Ongoing Pulpit Supply. Often these terms are used interchangeably, resulting in a blurring of the distinction between them. Yet the distinctions are significant.

For the sake of clarity, the initial letter in the titles Interim Pastor, Intentional Interim Pastor, Transitional Pastor and Ongoing Pulpit Supply will be capitalized when referring to these specific roles in transitional ministry, to help emphasize the distinction between them. When I'm referring to interim or transitional ministry in more generic terms, without differentiating between these specific roles, small case initial letters will be used.

When I was first starting out in ministry (it seems like a thousand years ago, but it was only in the early sixties), there was, and still is, a need for pulpit supply. Pulpit supply is usually limited to filling the pulpit (preaching) on a very short-term basis. There was no expectation of a continuous, formal relationship between the person filling the pulpit and the congregation. The congregation usually had a settled pastor who was gone for a week or two and would be returning in short order.

At that time, if someone was going to be filling a pulpit for an extended time because the settled pastor was ill or because the church was between settled pastors, they were called a transitional pastor. I refer to this position now as "Ongoing Pulpit Supply." Ongoing Pulpit Supply indicates someone who is at a church on a continuing basis. The relationship may or may not be formalized with a written agreement. In addition to performing Sunday services, that person might also cover funerals and perhaps weddings. Other than fulfilling these roles, churches usually don't expect much else from the Ongoing Pulpit Supply.

Let me propose a football analogy: Think of the Ongoing Pulpit Supply as the equivalent of the grounds crew. They're important to prepare the field for the game, but they aren't focused on the players or the outcome of the game after the kickoff. This person doesn't interact with the congregation much outside of a formal worship service. Some congregations say they're looking for a transitional pastor when what they actually want is to be sure someone fills the pulpit (Ongoing Pulpit Supply) while the search for a settled pastor is in progress.

An Interim Pastor, on the other hand, holds the space of a pastor. They're expected to keep things going until the new pastor arrives on the scene. This is more than providing a Sunday morning sermon. It involves basic pastoral care of the congregation (including hospital calls and shut-in visitation) and perhaps some guidance in various committee, team, or board meetings. There's no sense that the Interim Pastor should be facilitating the progress of the church, either spiritually or numerically, other than getting the congregation to progress toward calling a new pastor.

Returning to the football analogy, one way to understand the Interim Pastor is to see their position as similar to the half-time show at a football game. The halftime program is usually predictable and doesn't really have an effect on the game. However, it serves an important function: keeping the crowd warmed up and entertained while the teams take a break to rest and strategize.

The more formal term of Interim Pastor is used to refer to a person acting in the role of pastor of a congregation while a search for a settled pastor is in progress. It's normal for the Interim Pastor to have a recognized ordination, but they may not have any specialized training as a transitional pastor. This doesn't mean the person isn't competent. They may do the job very well.

A Transitional Pastor, on the other hand, shepherds a congregation through the interval between the ending of one settled pastorate and the beginning of a new settled pastorate. There may be specific tasks to be done and, in many cases, the success of the next pastor may depend on how well the transitional pastor does their job. The Transitional Pastor helps a congregation clarify what the congregation is looking for. If a congregation isn't really aware of what they need in a settled pastor, they'll be less likely to call a pastor who can move them forward.

The Transitional Pastor is very similar to the Interim Pastor, but the Transitional Pastor is focused on helping the congregation move from one phase of its life into another phase. This means an awareness of the changes taking place within the church and preparing the congregation for what will come next. They'll act as support for the congregation as they work their way through the process.

In the football analogy, I liken the Transitional Pastor to the trainers and assistant coaches. They're very hands-on and the team's ability to function into the future depends on their actions.

The Intentional Interim Pastor is similar to the Transitional Pastor, but has the added advantage of being trained in a specific process to lead a congregation through an exploration of their identity as a church as a prelude to calling a settled pastor. The level of training may vary. I received my training from the Center for Congregational Health after having already completed some interim assignments. The Interim Ministry Network provides continuing education and recognition of people who are trained as Intentional Interim Pastors. I believe I offered my best in each instance where I served as a Transitional Pastor, but I could have offered much more as an Intentional Interim Pastor.

The Intentional Interim Pastor not only helps a congregation clarify what they want from a future settled pastor, but they lead the congregation in a journey of self-discovery. The congregation comes to a clearer understanding of who they want as a pastor, as well as who they are and how that has led them to the desire they have for a settled pastor.

In addition, the Intentional Interim Pastor will look at how things are operating in the church and make suggestions for changes to help the next settled pastor. These can be changes in how finances are handled, the by-laws of the group, the functioning of various ministries within the church, or how the worship service functions.

In the football analogy, the Intentional Interim Pastor is the head coach for the church during the time it's searching for a settled pastor. The head coach has to see the larger picture and prepare the team to make changes in the game plan as new situations develop.

There's a great demand for people to serve as pastors during the time between settled pastors. Many pastors who retire from a settled position seek to do interim ministry. Some denominations would be in big trouble if not for these people who are filling in the gaps. But don't confuse that form of interim ministry with Intentional Interim Ministry or Transitional Ministry.

If a church is looking for an Ongoing Pulpit Supply or Interim Pastor, there are two tasks for denominational leadership: First, the denomination must have materials available for the church to help guide them in the search for a settled pastor. The most common materials the denomination will have will include a statement of policies the denomination has, a guide book regarding the helpful steps a church must take and guidelines about salary and other compensation related to the ministry. This book would be another possible resource.

Second, the denomination must have a list of names ready, so that when a congregation calls, the denominational leadership can recommend persons who are a good match for a particular congregation. It's important to avoid a mismatch that may result in conflict or the separation of the congregation from the denomination. In this instance, most of the work related to calling a settled pastor will fall solely on the congregation. The Interim Pastor or Ongoing Pulpit Supply will remain outside the whole search and call process.

The Transitional Pastor adds another dimension for the denominational leadership to be aware of. For one thing, the denominational leadership needs to be aware of whether or not the Transitional Pastor knows how to help a congregation clarify and state what it wants in a pastor. Denominational leadership should also have resources available for the Transitional Pastor to use in helping the congregation state its desires.

That being said, no matter how prepared a denominational office is, there will always be the potential for mismatches in calling either a settled pastor or a transitional pastor to a particular congregation. Perhaps it's a function of human nature, but I firmly believe that careful consideration on the part of a congregation will result in a better fit with a transitional pastor as well as with a settled pastor, and there will be fewer difficulties down the road.

My hope is that denominational leadership will facilitate a congregation's consideration of an Intentional Interim Pastor or Transitional Pastor over other forms of interim work. In many churches, the idea of a Transitional Pastor or Intentional Interim Pastor is new. The first step is to educate churches regarding these concepts and how they may help a church prepare for a new settled pastor. As it is, when a congregation finds itself without a settled pastor, there's a certain amount of panic or anxiety involved. If their reaction isn't focused on anything other than "getting a pastor," the result will likely be unhealthy. If the congregation's anxiety is understood, taken into consideration, and seen as a larger part of the history of the church, then that anxious energy can be motivating and health-producing. The more attention paid to these transitional roles, the better the chances are that a church will find a good fit with their next settled pastor.

Chapter 4:
First Things First

During Transitional Periods, Churches are in Trauma

During a time of transition, congregations aren't the same as usual—they're in a state of trauma. Working in a trauma situation is much different from serving a church in a settled pastoral situation. There are a variety of ways to understand what trauma is. The Merriam Webster online dictionary says the following: [2]

> "Definition of trauma
> 1a: an injury (such as a wound) to living tissue caused by an extrinsic agent
> b: a disordered psychic or behavioral state resulting from severe mental or emotional stress or physical injury
> c: an emotional upset"

In most congregations, a pastor is the spiritual leader of the congregation. As such, the congregation looks to the pastor as an indication of God's love and presence in their life. Even if a pastor isn't liked, there's still a sense that the pastoral presence gives safety. A congregation knows what to expect. They may not *like* what will happen, but they find security in predictable routines. Once the pastoral presence is removed, there's a vacuum.

2   https://www.merriam-webster.com/dictionary/trauma

Obviously, different congregations will react with differing degrees of emotional upset or stress. How a congregation reacts depends in part on the history of the church in dealing with change. If they've had good success with change in the past, the trauma will likely be minimized. If they've had trouble with change in the past, the trauma will be more severe. It comes down to their sense of being vulnerable or secure amidst the events that are unfolding.

Be aware that I'm vastly simplifying the concept of trauma. When a person or congregation has been traumatized, it means they've lost the usual indicators of safety. For them, the world is unsafe and unpredictable. Human beings—whether it be an individual or a group such as a congregation—demonstrate common reactions to feeling unsafe in an unpredictable environment. Group dynamics complicate the situation because each individual will bring with them different responses in varying degrees.

There are different indicators of an individual having been traumatized. These include emotional and psychological symptoms such as: shock, denial or disbelief, confusion, difficulty concentrating, anger, irritability, mood swings, anxiety and fear, guilt, shame, self-blame, withdrawing from others, feeling sad or hopeless, feeling disconnected or numb.[3] There may also be physical symptoms including: insomnia or nightmares, fatigue, being startled easily, difficulty concentrating, racing heartbeat, edginess and agitation, aches and pains, and muscle tension.

Some of these symptoms, both the psychological and physical symptoms, may be observed directly in congregations that have recently lost a pastor. Not every symptom will be in every

---

3   https://www.helpguide.org/articles/ptsd-trauma/coping-with-emotional-and-psychological-trauma.htm

congregation, and it may be easier to spot these symptoms in an individual than it is to spot them in a group as a whole.

The more common symptoms I've personally noted in congregations are: shock, denial or disbelief, confusion, difficulty concentrating, irritability, anxiety and fear, guilt, shame, self-blame, withdrawing from others, feeling sad or hopeless, feeling disconnected or numb, fatigue, being startled easily, and edginess or agitation. I will address a few of these.

One way people deal with loss is to deny it really happened. Congregations can't really deny that a pastor—who they may have viewed as the physical representation of God in the church—is gone. What they *can* do is deny their reactions. You might see this symptom in a congregation's resistance to discussing the former pastor. There may also be a general resistance or a specific resistance to discussing things that did not go well in the past.

The denial of what happened can often result in the congregation keeping in direct contact with the former pastor, even if the pastor has moved away. A very serious problem that transitional pastors face is when the former pastor keeps exerting influence over the congregation. In that case, both the congregation, or some portion of it, and the former pastor are in denial of what has occurred. One reason for insisting on cutting all ties with the former pastor is to overcome the denial that anything has really changed. The same applies to a transitional pastor: it's important to cut all ties, at least for a time, once the interim period is over.

Another form of denial comes in the form of assuming (or insisting) the former pastor's actions are the default—the way they performed their role is the yardstick by which all future actions are measured. This denies the truth that there is more than "one right way" to do something.

A congregation may also show signs of difficulty concentrating. They may find that things that were simple or routine now require a lot more effort. Tasks may be started and left unfinished.

A congregation may also become more irritable. This may be noted in different members of the congregation expressing animosity with one another. This isn't always done openly. Members may withdraw from one another, particularly if one segment of the congregation blames another segment for the pastor's departure.

Perhaps the most common indication a congregation is suffering from trauma is anxiety. Congregations may become concerned whether or not they'll be able to survive. Some of those concerns are real, but the extent of the anxiety will be greater than the facts support.

Anxiety can trigger a desperate push to get a new settled pastor in place. Consciously or unconsciously, the drive is to get things back to "normal." That may mean that the person the church approaches about being the next settled pastor could be someone who closely mimics the former pastor. It's rare for a congregation to see they're trying to select someone who's similar to the former pastor. Congregants will point out cosmetic differences and miss seeing underlying similarities of attitude.

It's also common for a transitional pastor to be asked if they could stay on as pastor. This is also a result of anxiety on the part of those asking. Congregants develop a sense of safety with the interim and are then fearful of losing that security when the interim leaves.

When a pastor leaves, there are often several people in the congregation who also leave. This may be an attempt on their part to avoid the anxiety of worshiping where they have to adjust to a new pastor. They may also leave out of denial. If they leave, in their minds nothing has really changed in the church.

Depending on the circumstances of the pastor's leaving, there can be a lot of guilt, shame, and self-blame that manifests. In cases where there was some form of misconduct on the pastor's part, these symptoms are usually lessened but not gone entirely. A congregation may blame itself for not having seen the "writing on the wall" and acting to change the situation.

In cases where there isn't misconduct, the congregation may blame themselves for not doing more to make the pastor want to stay: increased attendance, better salary, or offering support for the pastor's suggested programs. The self-blame can result in shame or guilt. Guilt manifests when the congregation believes they, as a whole, have done something specifically "bad." If they believe they, as a whole, are simply no good, then it becomes shame.

Another sign of trauma is unrelenting fatigue. In a church setting, it will show up in people unwilling to take on important roles in the congregation. There can be fatigue related to too few people doing too much, but trauma fatigue is more than that. Trauma fatigue results in important tasks going undone and minor, insignificant tasks becoming the focus of the work in the church.

The exaggerated startle response is one of the most popularly recognized features of PTSD. Soldiers returning from a war zone may show an increased startle response when a door bangs shut. They may react as if they were in combat, by taking cover or physically assaulting someone near them. The trauma that a congregation feels at the loss of their pastor is nowhere near the level of trauma experienced by veterans returning from war, but there can be a similar startle response. The congregation may be vigilant for any indication someone else is going to leave the church. If someone expresses displeasure, then other members may react with near-panic, rushing to make changes and alleviate any displeasure. Their focus is placed on keeping everyone satisfied, an impossible task.

If there are specific factors that contributed to a pastor leaving a church, then anytime those factors show up, the congregation will react as if they're again losing their pastor. One good reason to talk from the beginning about the transitional pastor being temporary is to normalize the transitional process and relieve the trauma associated with the departure of a pastoral presence.

A primary focus of the interim minister will be to facilitate the congregation feeling safe once more. I use the word "facilitate" rather than "help" intentionally. In my way of understanding, "helping" means to be personally involved and actively taking part in what needs to be done. "Facilitating" is a matter of making it possible for someone else to do what needs to be done. One of my goals as a transitional minister is to leave a congregation standing on their own feet—able to see that their security is a result of what *they* do, not of someone else holding them up.

One final word of warning: In psychology there's some emphasis on "secondary PTSD." One way this shows up is when a clinician begins to experience symptoms similar to the patient, even though the clinician hasn't been directly exposed to the same trauma. The exposure to the trauma comes in dealing with the patient.

It's possible for the interim minister to also suffer a secondary trauma when dealing with a congregation. One way of knowing that's happening is when the interim feels more anger at the situation than is warranted. It may be anger at the congregation, the former pastor, or at individuals in the congregation or community who are perceived as having been a part of the former pastor's departure.

Another indication of secondary PTSD is the interim minister becoming "hyper-vigilant" of what is being said amongst the congregation. The tendency to interpret statements, or actions, as being directed at the interim may mean that secondary trauma is setting in.

Giving Surveys

During periods of transition, a common practice is to give a survey to the church asking what congregants want in a new pastor. While this may be helpful, it can also be unhelpful to the process. There can often be a major disconnect between what a congregation thinks they want and what they actually need. This disconnect comes out of preconceived notions about what a pastor should be. The surveys I've seen tend to be answered more from the perspective of what a church thinks it *should* want in a pastor. In that context, it's hard to struggle with what the church truly needs, if that need doesn't fit the church's preconceived notions of what defines a "good" pastor.

In instances like these, I'm reminded of premarital counseling. There are many surveys that ask people what they want in an ideal partner. However, the answers often reflect what the individual thinks they are supposed to answer. This results from a lack of knowing oneself.

Dr. Aaron Beck wrote a book called *Cognitive Marital Counseling*. He pointed out that couples will often say a specific characteristic attracts them to each other, but in the end that very thing is what irritates them most about one another. For example, a man might say he appreciates a good homemaker. Later in life, he might complain that his partner isn't any fun because his spouse is *so* focused on the home they don't go out anymore. A woman, on the other hand, may say she wants a provider. Later on, she's upset because her spouse puts work ahead of everything else. While these are stereotypes and exaggerations to some degree, they do realistically reflect how we say we want one thing and when we get it, we end up frustrated.

In my experience with churches, the top answers on these surveys are always very similar: 1) There's a desire for bringing people into the church, particularly young people; 2) There's a desire for someone to perform pastoral care; 3) There's a desire for someone to work with the youth. While the exact order and content of the "wants" in a new pastor may vary, these three are almost always a given. That means the survey doesn't really provide any new information.

Churches may also say on surveys they want a particular *type* of pastor. But what they may not realize is that *that* particular type of pastor may come with baggage they don't really want. If they say they're looking for a young pastor, it's helpful to know *why* they want a young pastor. Is it to attract other young people into the community, or is it because they want the pastor to have a lot of energy to work for the church? Does the church realize what they're giving up in calling a young pastor? That pastor won't have the experience of someone who's been in ministry longer. Is the church able to be patient with a young pastor as they make the unavoidable mistakes which will provide them with the experience needed to be an effective pastor?

It's also a common complaint among pastors that the way the church presents itself during the interview process doesn't reflect what the church is actually like. I would posit that, in most cases, it isn't an intentional subterfuge on the part of the church. The church simply doesn't understand who they are and how to present themselves authentically.

Establishing the Ground Rules for Service

There are several things that need to be set in place before an interim minister can start their work. If attention is given to these, the interim's time of service will be much easier. This is not an exhaustive list of everything that should be considered, but these are areas that are commonly overlooked.

Power Structures in the Church

How an individual relates to the leadership and power structures in the church is important because that relationship also sets the stage for future interactions with a settled pastor. In my denomination, each church is autonomous. That means the structure of governance will be different from congregation to congregation. When I began in ministry, I could be safe in assuming there would be deacons, trustees, and various boards (Christian education, missions, etc.). That is no longer a safe assumption. I've served churches that no longer have any boards. Instead they use a "team" structure. At first

I assumed that was mainly a change in name. That isn't necessarily so. There may be a fundamental difference in understanding how teams function compared to a board.

Back in the early sixties, I could safely assume the deacons were the main body overseeing the general welfare of the church. Now there are churches that don't even have deacons. Some churches now have elders who take on many of the responsibilities that were once in the purview of the deacons.

There are also churches that have neither deacons nor elders. It may be a church council that makes ongoing decisions for a church, and the makeup of the church council can vary. It may be individuals who are elected by the congregation. It may also be people who are the heads of the different church boards or the chairperson of the various teams.

It also isn't unusual for there to be major issues in a church related to power structures. I used to think that people in churches were spiritually motivated and above the issues of power. ("When I was a child I reasoned like a child." 1 Corinthians 13:11) The reality is that people in churches behave just like people who aren't in churches. Everyone has a need for some sense of control or power in their life. Power is related to a person's basic survival instincts. If someone has no power, instinct tells them they won't survive long.

In any church, there will be established power structures. If a person comes into a church in an interim capacity and unwittingly interferes with the power structure, it can be disastrous. Sometimes there may be a *need* to change the power structures in a church to prepare for calling a settled pastor; but these changes need to be made intentionally and with forethought.

One reason for paying careful attention to negotiations before beginning work is that it establishes clear boundaries. Setting boundaries helps to recognize the power structures in a church and how to work within those structures, or how to change those structures. Negotiating a contract can also set a good example for the next pastor and may lessen the potential conflicts the incoming person will have.

Who Do You Negotiate With?

It's important to establish who the person, committee, board, or group is who has final say in various situations. In my experience, it could be the pastoral relations committee, a subcommittee of the church board, the moderator, or the deaconate. What's stated in the church by-laws might not, in fact, be the reality. It's critical to know who to go to when issues arise.

An interim won't carry the same authority as a settled pastor. In Baptist circles, a church vote is usually required to hire a pastor. However, since an interim is temporary, the hiring may be done by a smaller group within the church. I've had the problem where one group did the hiring and negotiating of the interim contract, but once there, I discovered that a different person was understood to be the "supervisor" of the Interim Pastor.

Who has authority is important to know for several reasons. There will always be issues that arise that aren't clearly associated with a particular person or group in the church. It's important to know who to go to for clarification. For example, if the interim wants to take vacation time or wants to attend a continuing education event, it's usually expected that the interim will need to seek approval. It doesn't help to get approval from the wrong person, and it's easy to set up unnecessary conflict by getting permission from the wrong person. There have been cases where one person seemed to be the person to negotiate with, only to find out later that there was a specific board or person who expected to give the approval.

Issues may also arise that weren't formally negotiated. It saves time and trouble if the interim knows who to go to in order to renegotiate issues that have been overlooked or weren't part of the original contract. Approval from the wrong person or board can be worse than no approval at all.

In some cases, you'll find a church doesn't fully understand its own power structures. There was a church I once served as a settled pastor that wanted to bring in a guest speaker. I went to the board of deacons, assuming they were overseeing the spiritual wellbeing of the church. They had no objection, but one of the deacons said the decision was really up to the trustees since they'd have to approve paying for the person's expenses. I took the proposal to the board of trustees and they had no objections. However, they suggested I really needed to get permission from the board of Christian education, because the person coming in would be informing us about some mission issues in our area. The board of Christian education didn't object, but said the permission should come from the board of missions. Again, the issue was kicked to another board. The person I was bringing in was a woman who was an associate pastor in a sister church in the area. The board of missions had no objection to a woman speaking, but this woman was a pastor. So they suggested I take the matter to the board of deaconesses (all women). Finally, I had approval of all the boards.

Power, or *who* could do *what*, was a serious issue in that church. At times it prevented them from accomplishing important goals. However, to be honest, once a decision was reached, there was little conflict or disagreement about what had been decided. I haven't had any interim position that was as convoluted as that one, but it did teach me to pay attention to the issues of power and hierarchy within a congregation.

Expectations Regarding the Amount of Services Provided

An interim position can be full-time or part-time. If full-time, there may be less discussion regarding the amount of service to be expected, unless the former pastor was overworked. However, if it's a part-time position, there needs to be a clear understanding of how much time will be devoted to performing the transitional pastor's duties. It's easy for a congregation to *say* they realize a part-time person won't be available as much as their former pastor. However, words don't always match expectations. There can be a lot of time wasted over arguing about the hours.

One way of attending to this problem is for the interim to keep track of their actual hours worked. I personally find this to be a difficult approach. One problem is that a significant amount of time can be used up just keeping a record of hours. One is also faced with the difficulty of deciding what to do with partial hours. At first glance, it seems straightforward, but in practice it's complicated.

A second approach is to agree to a number of days, usually with the days specified. This is preferable to hours because the interim doesn't have to try to limit their time. The problem is that there may be special services (e.g., funerals) that might occur on days other than the agreed-upon days. There can also be a problem with how much work needs to be crammed into a single day. There's a major difference between working the equivalent of an eight-hour day and the equivalent of a thirteen- or fourteen-hour day.

For me, the most useful approach is to use "units of service," where morning, afternoon, and evening are each one unit. If the interim agrees to three days a week, it would mean six to nine total units. I prefer this method because it's the least complicated. The units can be flexible to accommodate situations that call for a transitional pastor to be available at a time other than their regular schedule. When negotiating a contract, I contract for a specific number of units per week.

Remember that one thing the Transitional Pastor or Intentional Interim Pastor does is establish expectations the church will have of the incoming settled pastor. If the Transitional Pastor works way more than they originally agreed upon, the church will expect the same of a settled pastor.

Holidays

It's easy to forget to include holidays in pre-start negotiations. Holidays exist for a reason. We all need regular times to recharge. A holiday breaks up the routine and can be even more refreshing than a vacation.

It needs to be clear if the interim is expected to work on holidays. Many holidays in the United Sates fall on Mondays. If the interim normally works on Mondays, and Monday is a holiday, are they still expected to be present at the church? If the interim isn't expected to work on holidays, are they paid for those holidays if they fall on days normally worked? It may seem the answer is obvious, but it isn't always clear. The results of your individual negotiations can be spelled out in a contract or in a letter of understanding.

In some part-time positions, the interim isn't expected to work on holidays, but the time is expected to be made up later. While this may make sense from a business model, it also abrogates the value of holidays. If it is indeed to be a holiday, then it needs to be paid.

Vacation Time

Related to holidays is the issue of vacation time. This is particularly important if you're part-time. Interim work can be more stressful than people realize. One approach is to offer a week of paid vacation each quarter. Note that I said *paid* vacation. Sometimes people want to say, "Sure, take the week," but they don't expect to pay for it. This is particularly true if you're part-time. The problem is that if the time isn't paid, then there's a financial incentive to *not* take vacations. If there isn't time for the interim to recharge, the quality of their work will suffer and the interim may become burned out.

Related to this is establishing *when* you take the vacation. It's usually expected that you won't take vacation during major religious holidays or major church events. However, the church might expect a full quarter to pass before any vacation can be taken. That needs to be clarified in negotiations.

Another part of the negotiations might include whether or not the vacation time can accrue and, if so, how much? It needs to be clear how many vacation days can be accrued and if there are any restrictions as to when they are used, including how many days can be strung together.

Denomination Meetings and Involvement

It's also important that denominational meetings are included as paid work days. It's better if there's some specificity regarding what is or isn't a denominational event. These events could include conventions (national or regional), meetings with other clergy, tasks that are specifically requested by the denominational leaders, as well as others. Don't forget that denominational affiliations might include minister council meetings.

Be sure to clarify if any fees, travel expenses, and other costs associated with a denominational event will be paid by the church.

Salary

Salary depends on how much time is expected from a transitional pastor. If the former pastor was "full-time," and if the church expects the interim to put in an equivalent amount of time, then the salary should at least be whatever the salary (including all compensation) was of the former settled pastor. If the interim is to be less than full-time, then the salary can be set based on a percentage of time that the full-time pastor received.

It's obvious that salary should be negotiated before work starts. It may be based on a general figure for doing the work, on units of work done, or even on hours (which I strongly recommend against). A general suggestion for Intentional Interim Minsters is that the salary package be the same as it was for the former pastor. This may help avoid a situation where an interim minister costs less for the church, and then hiring a settled pastor entails increasing costs for the church. Also, if there's a lower salary paid to the interim, a church may drag its feet on finding a settled pastor as a cost reduction strategy.

Another aspect of salary negotiation is *when* the salary is paid. Is it weekly, biweekly, or monthly? Related to this is what form of paper work (if any) the pastor needs to provide. Some churches require a form that lists some of the pastor's activities for the time period they're being paid for. Other churches don't ask for anything and just make the payment as a routine action. It also needs to be clear who writes the checks or arranges for automatic deposits. If a check is written, it needs to be understood where it will be left or if it will be mailed. If an automatic deposit is used, it needs to be clearly understood when that deposit will be made.

It's also helpful in the process of salary negotiation to address the issue of pay raises. I used to consider it unspiritual to talk about such things. What I discovered was that after a couple of years without a raise, I felt unappreciated.

Another reason to address the pay raise issue is that it's an important part of setting the stage for the settled pastor who will follow. Churches can be very unaware of the need for pay raises with a settled pastor and the interim can lead the way in enhancing that awareness.

Often, the interim won't be somewhere long enough for raises be an issue. But if the time extends to more than a year, then it is an issue. It's better if this is addressed at the beginning of the interim's tenure rather than trying to broach it later.

Expenses Paid by the Church

A transitional pastor's expenses should be paid. However, it's important that the amount paid and what is and isn't acceptable is established. What follows is a list of some common expenses. It isn't necessarily an exhaustive list.

- **Car expense:** What's the mileage rate and what are the limits (if any) on the number of miles to be reimbursed? How is the reimbursement handled—as a part of the regular pay check or as a separate check? What counts as a legitimate mileage expense as far as the church is concerned?

- **Hospitality:** There are times when a transitional pastor may need to cover the cost of a meal for a visitor or someone else who's helping the church. It's important that the circumstances of such expenses be clear and, if there are limits, that those limits be understood.

- **Program expense:** If the interim needs supplies or program materials, what are the limits and who gives approval?

- **Continuing education:** How much continuing education time is allowed? What days can be used for continuing education? Are registration fees paid? Is travel paid? Is room and board paid? Again, this is an important part of setting the stage for how the church will react to a settled pastor.

- **Dues:** Are dues to The Ministers Council and other such groups (local clergy associations) paid by the church?

How the transitional minister handles expenses—turning them in and expecting reimbursement—can affect how the church will react to a settled pastor. It's sometimes tempting to ignore some expenses, but in the end the interim will be doing a disservice to the church and the incoming pastor.

Termination Issues

How much time is allowed to finish up ministry before the interim leaves? Two weeks is a minimum and, in my opinion, not sufficient. Keep in mind that it may take several weeks or months for a new position for the interim to come open. There are arrangements where six- or eight-weeks' notice of termination of the contract is required by both parties. It should be understood that if the church wants to terminate the relationship before the time allotted, they can do so, but they should pay for the time even if it isn't used.

Obviously, in case of pastoral misconduct, termination should happen at once. However, that needs to be stated in the initial agreement.

There can also be a mutual agreement to terminate the contract on a schedule different from what was originally contracted. However, the agreement needs to be two-sided. What applies for one party also applies to the other party. For instance: If there's an eight-week contract and the church wants to terminate it after four weeks, then the remaining four weeks should still be paid. On the other hand, even if it's more convenient for the interim to leave after four weeks, the remaining four weeks of service should still be delivered with the same devotion to service as the interim had been giving previously.

I have included several examples of contracts in Appendix A.

Some General Issues

- **Endings:** Make it clear from the very beginning that you, as the interim, will be leaving. It's important to set the stage for leaving from the very beginning. I also recommend that the interim regularly—from the pulpit or in some other form of communication—remind the congregation that you are only there temporarily.

- **Worship:** Interim ministers often make changes in the worship service. I don't do that simply for the sake of making changes. However, I do use changes in the worship service as a way to prepare the congregation for a settled pastor. While some congregations are very comfortable with changes in the worship service, others aren't very amenable to change.

  If someone comes to me with a complaint about the changes I make, after genuinely listening and considering their feedback, I will usually tell them that each pastor will have preferences in how worship (or other church functions) should happen and that the new, settled pastor will undoubtedly have changes of their own to make. I also remind them that my changes are temporary because I am temporary.

- **Listening:** It's important to encourage people to come and talk to you as the interim about things they don't like. When they come, you have to be able to listen, really listen, without defending yourself. If you can be present with people and not attempt to tell them they are wrong, even if you believe they are, you will be building a relationship between the church and pastor which will last into the next pastorate. Ask people who have other congregation members complaining to them, to encourage the complaining party to come talk to you directly.

The Transition Team

There are two separate committees or teams that are important during the transition period. In my denominational background, one of these is called the "pastoral search committee" or the "pulpit committee" or some variation of the two. Most by-laws include a section on how to set up such a committee and perhaps how the committee is to function.

The second committee that's involved in the setting the stage for the calling of the new pastor is the "transition team" or the "transition committee." I prefer "transition team" because it's clearer the group will be working cooperatively and everyone will have their own part to play. They're not a group that sets agendas and then leaves the work to others. Committees are often, although not always, seen more as "governing" groups than "working" groups.

The transition team is a new concept in many churches in my denomination. I believe many new pastors face unexpected and unneeded difficulties because a church hasn't understood the need for and the function of the transition team.

The transition team helps the congregation explore who they are. One of the biggest dangers for a church is calling a new pastor based on what they think they "should" need and not on what they actually need. This may be because they're trying to appear spiritual, because they're trying to imitate other churches, or because they just don't understand themselves.

A transition team does the groundwork of preparing the church for the incoming settled pastor. It may include a careful examination of what the church needs to "fix" and what the needs of the church are before the new pastor is called. Another way of saying this with more emotional impact is to say that the transition team has the chance to make clear what is "broken" and what needs to be "fixed." This isn't to imply the transition team *determines* what is "broken," but the transition team can lead the congregation in exploring what needs to change.

I developed a survey (Appendix B) to give to the congregation. Based on that survey, the congregation can examine what needs to be paid attention to before a new settled pastor arrives. The transition team's role is to get the information out to the congregation.

While the exact function of the transition team will vary from church to church and from transitional pastor to transitional pastor, there are some things every transition team should pay attention to:

- The transition team should guide the church in exploring the Five Focus Points. They can decide which Focus Points need the most attention and how to see that all of the points are appropriately explored. The team can further make sure that the information obtained in exploring the Focus Points is disseminated through the entire congregation.

- The team should also make suggestions to the congregation about what needs to be changed. It's important to remember that these are only suggestions. The transition team shouldn't take it on themselves to *make* the changes. Once they've reported back to the congregation, directly or through the appropriate governing board, the action should be undertaken by the appropriate committee, board, or team.

- The transition team should also write up what they've worked with the church on and what suggestions they made, and make that information available to the incoming settled pastor. This information will give the new pastor a better picture of what the church is like and show that the church is ready, or not ready, to move forward.

It's always difficult to determine the make-up of the transition team. This is particularly true of these congregations which have not previously been acquainted with or used a transition team. In general, the team should consist of a representative section of the congregation. (Note the difference between "representative" and "represents.") It should be balanced in terms of gender, ethnicity, age (with an exception) and how long someone has been a part of the congregation. The age exception is for younger people, who are often ineffective. It is important that the team members be competent to do the tasks that are needed during the transition period. The team may have to make hard decisions and youth may be hesitant to speak up or may lack an understanding of the way the congregation functions.

The team needs to consist of people who are trusted by the rest of the congregation. If that trust is lacking, there may be resistance to anything the team suggests. Congregational input on who should make up the team is important. However, it needs to be understood by the congregation that this is a working team, not a "thinking" team. The transitional pastor should have major input into who is ultimately on the team.

"Transition Team" versus "Search Committee"

Most churches want to get a settled pastor as soon as possible. To facilitate that goal, they'll want to get a search committee in place at once, sometimes even before the outgoing pastor has left. This is a result of anxiety at being without a pastor, but it's best to establish the transition team first and give them time to work though understanding where the congregation is at and give them a chance to work through the Five Focus Points. Once this work is complete, then the search committee can be brought together.

A well-functioning transition team will make the work of the search committee much less burdensome. The development of the church profile in terms of who the congregation is and an understanding of what the church needs in a pastor will already be done. The search committee will be able to draw on this work as they put together a picture of the church to be distributed to candidates.

Many times, a search committee is tasked with putting together the entire church profile and deciding what the congregation wants in a pastor. This profile is usually heavy in terms of statistics and light in terms of the culture or internal workings of the congregation. Also, there can be a tendency for the committee to ask the members of the congregation what they "want" in a pastor. That question in survey form or discussion form will likely produce a consistent set of answers that may or may not be a true reflection of the congregation's needs.

Chapter 5:
The Interim's Mindset

SPIRITUAL MATTERS ARE ALWAYS PERSONAL. A pastor represents, correctly or incorrectly, an individual's spiritual life and is, perhaps, viewed to be an individual's representative before God. If there's no one in that role, congregants may feel extremely vulnerable. A major focus of interim ministry is securing the spiritual wellbeing of the individuals in the congregation.

If personal spiritual security is wrapped up with a figure out in front (a settled pastor), then there can be tremendous pressure to fill the vacancy. An interim may feel pressured to get the job done and facilitate the securing of the settled pastor as quickly as possible. This pressure to move quickly can be seen in different ways. One of the more common ways is for congregants to impatiently ask, "What is the search committee doing?"

This feeling of personal spiritual vulnerability, when widespread in a congregation, will sometimes move a church to call the first person who appears to lessen that feeling of vulnerability. A charismatic individual may sweep the congregation off their feet. However, if the candidate isn't a good fit with the congregation, the result can be very unsatisfying in the long-term for one or both parties.

To avoid (or lessen) the pressure created by feelings of personal vulnerability, individuals in a congregation will need to be reassured in two ways. First, they need assurance they haven't been abandoned by God or by the denomination. Second, the congregation will need to have hope things will settle down. That hope can't be given in words only. There's a need for experiences, personal individual experiences of congregants, that give hope.

There are different ways the individual experiences in dark times can be made evident. One way would be a retreat-type atmosphere[4] where the focus would be "How did you experience God's presence in your own dark times?" Another might be to dedicate a church newsletter to people sharing their experience of God's guidance and presence with them when things in general seemed darkest.

What can add to the difficulty of dealing with congregants' spiritual vulnerability is people who say they hold beliefs that, in actuality, they don't believe or at least believe in only limited ways. In congregational churches, for example, the accepted belief is usually that God is at work and the pastor is merely a servant of God and doesn't carry any special spiritual power. This isn't always what congregations actually believe, however. The pastor is often seen as God's representative and, as such, the lack of a pastor is in effect the lack of God.

Some individuals in a congregation may say, "God is in charge." What I have experienced is this phrase, when employed, reveals a working disconnect from the members of the congregation and God. They have learned knowledge (orthodoxy) of the Holy Spirit, but they have little to no knowledge based on practical experience (orthopraxis) with the Holy Spirit. Church is a place to go and "do," not a place to come and "experience."

---

4   I said "retreat-type atmosphere" because it doesn't have to be about going away somewhere. It's an atmosphere where people are welcome and where sharing of stories is encouraged, even if it is held at the church.

The "God is in charge" stance in the life of church members is sometimes accompanied by a false sense that no matter what, God will make things right. I do believe God will make things right; but that doesn't mean we aren't responsible for our actions. The Children of Israel first assumed their opinion was greater than God's and refused to advance into the Promised Land. When they were confronted by Moses with their lack of a willingness to follow where God led them, they assumed they could take the Promised Land even if God said no. We all know the results: forty years of wandering in the wilderness and the death of all those who were in leadership at the time, except for Joshua and Caleb.

The congregation may need to be educated about what the work of a transitional minister can mean. This can't be done while the congregation is in the psychological crisis that follows the leaving of a pastor, whether the pastor was loved or hated. The denominational leadership can be most helpful if they begin this educational process before there's the possibility of a pastor leaving. Of course, it may be that the first thing the denominational leadership hears is that the pastor has left or will be leaving. This precludes a long education process. If that's the case, it would be best to meet with the congregation as soon as possible and explain the difference between the types of interim ministry the congregation can contract with. This would mean slowing down the rush to get another pastor. It might mean the interim will need to help the church see that the church moving forward is ultimately the responsibility of the members of the congregation and that some degree of health is needed before the church calls a settled pastor.

If the congregation hasn't yet established a search committee, it would be helpful for them to delay doing so until an interim is in place and has had a chance to work with them. If the congregation has already established a search committee, it would be helpful to put all of that activity on hold. The reason for this is that once a search committee is in place, the congregation has already made some decisions about what kind of a pastor they're looking for. Those decisions are made by virtue of who was selected for the search committee.

Uniqueness of Transitional Pastors and Intentional Interim Pastors

Not everyone is trained to do the work of the Transitional Pastor or Intentional Interim Pastor. The job of the Intentional Interim Pastor or the Transitional Pastor is very different from the job of a settled pastor. When looking for a Transitional Pastor or an Intentional Interim Pastor, there can be a tendency to select someone who was a successful pastor and is retired. At other times, there may be a push to put someone who's looking for a settled pastorate into that role until a "real" calling comes about. Someone who has been a settled pastor may make a good Intentional Interim Pastor or Transitional Pastor, but they need to get additional training and mentoring. The two jobs aren't the same.

Sometimes a settled pastor will experience deep personal trauma in a congregation. There may be a perfectly natural desire on the part of denominational leadership to help the pastor heal and, as a result, they may move them into an interim position in another congregation. However, putting them into an interim position can result in the pastor's troubles contaminating their new situation. There are some pastors who can keep their issues separate from an interim position, but they are few.

As I said earlier, I started my ministry doing work as an Ongoing Pulpit Supply. If that's all a congregation needs, then it can be a good training ground for someone new to ministry. However, if there have been problems in the congregation, or if the congregation has a habit of chewing up and spitting out pastors, a person just starting in ministry may be scarred for life.

Intentional Interim Ministry and Transitional Ministry from a Consultation Model

A person may agree that the need for an Intentional Interim Pastor is great and understand they offer special skills a church will benefit from. The problem is there aren't enough people properly trained to do this kind of work. When congregations are without a pastor, there's a rush to alleviate the congregation's anxiety by connecting them with someone. Often the "someone" isn't trained in Intentional Interim Ministry or Transitional Ministry.

Denominational leaders are confronted with a dilemma when there are a dozen or more churches looking for an interim and there are only three or four people with formal training. The fallback position is to secure whomever is available so the congregation can feel like things are still under control. If the interim isn't trained in Intentional Interim Ministry, the results may be less than desirable, even if the person who goes to that congregation has been an exceptional settled pastor.

When there isn't a trained person available to work exclusively with one church, an alternative may be to have people trained in Intentional Interim Ministry meet with congregations who are already working with an Interim Pastor, Transitional Pastor, or even an Ongoing Pulpit Supply. This person could act as an Intentional Interim Consultant to a church transition committee or team. It wouldn't be a full-time position. The Intentional Interim Consultant would meet with the church very early in the process to explain the process and to facilitate the establishment of a transitional committee or team. Over a period of several months, the Intentional Interim Consultant would meet regularly with a congregational transition committee and help them find ways to do the self-examination process.

A weekly or monthly meeting time would be established and the Intentional Interim Consultant would devote time to the church at those meetings. This wouldn't mean the consultant would be filling the pulpit every Sunday. The consultant might only fill the pulpit occasionally to bring focus on the next stage of the church's self-examination process.

Assuming there's an Ongoing Pulpit Supply, Interim Pastor, or Transitional Pastor in place, there would need to be a close working relationship between that person and the consultant. The Ongoing Pulpit Supply, Interim Pastor, or Transitional Pastor would have to trust the process the consultant would be leading the church through.

An issue that the church would have to face is that an Intentional Interim Consultant would mean additional expense for the congregation. There would need to be a consultant fee paid as well as expenses, such as mileage. Other related expenses would need to be reimbursed as well.

One the other hand, if a church moves ahead without really understanding who they are and what they need in a settled pastor who will match the personality of the church, the cost will be even greater in the long run. Without carefully considered action in seeking a settled pastor, there will be a greater risk of hurts within the congregation, short-term pastorates, and general frustration and disappointment with the church.

Chapter 6:
The Effect of Perceptions of Former Pastors

HOW A CHURCH WILL REACT TO a Transitional Pastor depends in part on their experience with the former pastor. It's important to know how the former settled pastor was perceived by the congregation. If the interim isn't aware of how the congregation's reaction to them is shaped by the former settled pastor, there will be a lot of unnecessary hurt and frustration. Adjusting your behavior to the congregation's previous experience is vital.

This doesn't mean the interim should be anything less than authentic. The most useful tool an interim has is their own genuine presence. If the interim abandons who they are, it will negatively affect their work with the congregation. Still, the interim can be true to who they are and also tailor their interactions to suit the situation.

In any situation where an interim ministry is taking place, there's almost assuredly a variety of perceptions and opinions about the former settled pastor. Those perceptions can range from positive (almost idolizing) to negative (almost demonizing). While one perception may be predominating, most congregations will run the gamut (although the extremes at either end may not be present).

For convenience, I'll refer to those with a negative view of the former pastor as "con-former pastor" and those with a positive view as "pro-former pastor." When I hear any one perception, pro or con, I always assume there will be others who see things differently. A major part of the interim's role is to hear the different perceptions while not joining one side or another.

The people the transitional pastor will be interacting with will each have their own perceptions of the transitional pastor as well as the former pastor. Some church members can be insecure enough that they'll insist everyone must agree with their perspective. If the transitional pastor doesn't enthusiastically support their position, then they'll see the interim as the enemy. In that case, it does little good to try to affirm that you (the interim) aren't on one side or the other. Nevertheless, it still needs to be stated that the interim is neutral, but it will seldom be believed just because the interim says so. Actions, not words, will be believed.

Negatively-Perceived Former Pastors

Situations where the majority of the congregation are con-former pastor won't mean that *everyone* is con-former pastor. However, if the majority view is that the former pastor was in the wrong, then this will be the starting point for the interim's work.

When going to a church where there have been issues with a former pastor, it's safe to assume there will be an attempt to co-opt the interim into a position either for or against the former pastor.

The con-former pastor group may view everything the interim does through their experience of the former pastor. Any action the interim takes may be criticized and seen as "bad," but this isn't done out of malice. When someone has been hurt by an experience, there are psychological shifts that take place. People will seek to protect themselves from further harm. That reaction is important to an individual's survival and not an act of evil in and of itself. Thus, the congregation may unfairly make judgments about the behavior of the interim.

The behaviors of the former pastor are often projected onto the interim. We humans are very complicated. We use previous experiences to make decisions just to get by day by day. Those previous experiences or perceptions will of necessity be incomplete. A trivial example involves a stop light. When the light turns green, previous experience tells us the people driving on the cross street are basically law-abiding people. Due to that expectation, we proceed through the intersection. Sometimes we realize our projections may be wrong and wait to see if the other cars are really going to stop. Generally, however, we act on what has been true in the past.

For those who are con-former pastor, they are predisposed to negative assumptions about a transitional pastor. Again, this isn't an intentionally evil act. It's a natural reaction of the human personality. As an interim, it's best to behave in such a way that those who make the negative projections begin to question their projections. In the midst of those projections, the interim dare not take it personally.

If the transitional pastor does get sucked into the drama surrounding the negative opinion of the former pastor, the transitional pastor will lose effectiveness with those who were either pro-former pastor or neutral toward the former pastor. The issues that drove the former pastor to resign will most likely be perpetuated.

Positively-Perceived Former Pastors

The other side of the coin is the pro-former pastor group. They will also view the interim's actions with suspicion. In this case, however, the suspicion may be that the interim is responsible for dethroning the former settled pastor. The interim may not have known the congregation at all when the former pastor left, but that doesn't make a lot of difference. The pro-former pastor group thinks: If the interim wasn't here, the former pastor might still be here.

Another aspect of this involves the idea that the pro-former pastor group has made a commitment to the former pastor. This group usually sees themselves as loyal supporters and that it's their spiritual duty to maintain that support. They may believe that if they acknowledge any good came from the former pastor leaving, then they are in effect judging themselves to be spiritually defective. If they support anything the interim is doing, or support the transitional pastor in any way, they may perceive themselves to be "unfaithful" to a good former pastor.

Walking the Fine Line

To be effective, the interim must be able to work with both groups. That means being honest about what they see and what they don't see in terms of behavior and attitude on both sides of the street. More than likely, there will be some things the former pastor did that the interim can be supportive of, as well as some things the interim will be uncomfortable with. Ideally, the interim won't take sides and will remain completely neutral—but that would be a world that doesn't really exist. The best an interim can hope for is to find a balance between the two without going too far with negative or positive judgments.

Here's an important distinction: There may be *actions* the former pastor took that the interim believes were helpful, and also *actions* that the interim believes weren't helpful. The interim can make comments about actions, but avoid making it about the *person* of the former pastor. One possible way to approach this is say something like, "That's an action that I, personally, wouldn't do (or that I, personally, would do)." If at all possible, leave out any reference to the former pastor as an individual.

Those in the Middle

I have described two groups an interim might be faced with in a congregation: one group that's pro-former pastor and one group that's con-former pastor. There's almost always a third group. More often than not, the group in the middle is larger than either the pro or con groups, sometimes larger than the pro-former pastor group or the con-former pastor groups combined. This isn't a neutral group. It's a group with the attitude that whatever happened with the former pastor may or may not have been unfortunate, but they want to get on with the business of being servants of Jesus. For this group, the struggle between the pro-former pastor and the con-former pastor groups is a distraction. Their desire is usually to focus on where the church is going in the future.

It's always tempting to think the bulk of transitional work must be with this middle group. This third group will usually be supportive of the interim because they see the interim as leading the church to the "future" and away from the difficulties of the past.

Such support will usually feel pretty good to the interim. However, if the interim comes to revel in their support, there is the danger of ignoring the people in the pro or con groups who have issues that need to be addressed. Another problem is that strong congregational leadership will usually be found in the pro-former pastor or the con-former pastor groups, or in both. To ignore the leadership in ether of these groups isn't going to be healthy for the church.

A Positively-Perceived Former Pastor

When the former pastor was mostly positively-perceived, there are different issues that will need to be attended to during the interim. There will still be the pro-former pastor and con-former pastor groups, as well as those who are neither, but the impact on the transitional pastor will be different. Anything the interim does differently from the former pastor may be looked at as a betrayal of the former pastor. If not a betrayal, at least the difference may be viewed in a negative light.

The pro-former pastor group may know they have unreasonable expectations. They may be fully aware that it's unfair to project their hurt at the former pastor leaving (abandoning) them onto the interim. As a result, they may even feel some guilt for the way they approach the interim. However, that doesn't stop the projections.

An interim may end up dealing with people who seem resistant, but who also feel guilty about their resistance. It's helpful to establish that the interim is a different person than the former pastor and that, without condemning or negatively judging the former pastor, the interim will naturally do things differently.

In this positively-perceived former pastor scenario, the con-former pastor group will tend to be smaller and may feel that others think badly of them. At times they may be hostile because they think the people who liked the pastor blame *them* for the pastor leaving. They may want the interim to affirm that their reasons for disliking the pastor were valid. If the interim doesn't make such a clear affirmation, it can be easy for them to oppose the interim. They already have practice at opposing an otherwise-loved pastor.

Dealing with a Former Pastor's Boundary Violations

Boundary violations can take on different forms. Most people think of sexual harassment or similar indiscretions when it comes to a pastor violating boundaries. However, any time a trust is betrayed it's a form of a boundary violation. That can happen if funds are misused, if there's theft, if confidences are revealed, or if something else happens to violate the expected behavior of the pastor.

In cases where a former pastor violated boundaries, there will most certainly be mistrust of the transitional pastor. In this case, the interim's main goal is reestablishing the trust between the congregation and the pastor. That isn't something that can be done according to a particular formula. The transitional pastor has to avoid even the *appearance* of similar boundary violation issues. Note that I emphasize even the "appearance" of boundary issues. If the violation was of a sexual nature, the interim must be extra careful to not do anything that can be misinterpreted. Giving and receiving hugs is one example. Appropriate hugs can be healing, but if a former pastor violated sexual boundaries, then (at least initially) there's no hug that will be appropriate. Because sexuality was the focus of the former pastor's boundary violation, every action the interim takes will be seen through that lens.

Hugs can be very intimate, particularly if the hug appears to be last longer than expected because someone doesn't want to let go. Physical contact is always a risk. Don't assume it's okay if a congregant is the one who initiates the hug or intimate handshake. If there have been boundary violations, the transitional pastor is responsible for reestablishing clear boundaries.

A good rule when serving a church where there has been a boundary violation of a sexual nature is to not hug anyone. Even keep a handshake stiff and perfunctory. In some cases, a member of the church might reach out and hug the interim. It isn't helpful to protest that hugs are inappropriate. However, remaining more aloof than usual may send the message that hugs are not appropriate at the current time. Once the trust in the transitional pastor seems to be reestablished, hugs and handshakes can be more normal.

It's important to remember the interim might not intend to do anything wrong, but there may be some people who interpret even the most innocent of actions as sexual. Verbal protestations of your innocence aren't of much value. It's most likely that the former pastor, who *did* cross boundaries, also protested that they'd done nothing wrong.

At times there may be attempts to justify the former pastor's boundary violations on the basis of "love." These justifications send the message that the pastor had no control over the violation. That means, by implication, that *no one* can control actions based on "love." The way to rebuild trust in this scenario is to refuse to justify such actions for any reason at all. Keep in mind that actions speak louder than words. What the transitional pastor does will have more effect than what the transitional pastor says.

Even in cases of boundary violations, there will still be the pro-former pastor and the con-former pastor groups in the congregation. The con-former pastor group will be carrying a lot of anger and sometimes what is called "righteous indignation." This group will need to move toward forgiveness of the former pastor. Note the word is "forgiveness." That isn't to say the former pastor should be exonerated or that people should "let bygones be bygones" and close their eyes to what the pastor did. Yet, if those who carry anger aren't able to move beyond it, the church as a whole will suffer.

Even in cases of boundary violations, there will most likely be a pro-former pastor group. This group will be composed of people who held the offending pastor in high regard. They may carry a lot of anger toward anyone who initiated the actions leading to the pastor's departure. No matter what may be said, these people will believe the charges are a part of a conspiracy or that something else could have been done to keep the pastor from leaving.

The interim's goal with both of these groups is to leave them feeling they have been heard by the interim without judgment. That means a lot of active listening for the emotions people are carrying. Don't join in on the condemnation or the exoneration of the former pastor, it isn't helpful. Instead, try saying to both groups on a regular basis, "That must have really hurt you." People in both the pro-former pastor group and the con-former pastor group may come away from conversations thinking the interim is on their side.

Be sure they understand you're acknowledging their experiences, not the validity of their beliefs about the situation.

Dealing with Grief

One of the most difficult challenges is dealing with grief related to the former pastor. The exact reason for grief may vary. A pastor may have died, a pastor may have had health reasons for leaving, or a pastor may simply have felt it was time to move on to a different place of ministry. In some cases, the actual reasons for a pastor's departure may not be known by the congregation as a whole. (Some health conditions aren't released.) Not knowing *why* someone left makes the grieving process more difficult.

The main issue when dealing with grief comes down to uncertainty. By and large, we all want things to be somewhat predictable. Even if we don't like what happens, we'll feel better if we can see "why" it happened.

Any congregation dealing with grief issues—because of death or for some other reason—will need to work through the stages of grief. Typically, the stages of grief are identified as: 1) Denial: This cannot be real; 2) Anger: Striking back at someone or something because a person has been hurt; 3) Bargaining: Trying to make a deal which will change things back to how they were before whatever caused the grief; 4) Depression: Giving up and feeling totally defeated; 5) Acceptance of the situation and moving forward with life as it is.

It's important to understand that these things don't always happen in a linear fashion. Nor does working through one stage mean that it will never again have to be dealt with. Some stages are almost skipped over. Within a congregation, different people may be in different stages (and displaying the associated symptoms) of grief.

Chapter 7:
Working Toward the End

ONE DIFFERENCE BETWEEN A TRANSITIONAL PASTOR and a settled pastor is that interim ministry is a time-limited position. Some expect the time to be up to eighteen months, others see the time frame to be as much as twenty-four to thirty months. How long an interim position lasts will vary widely from person to person and church to church, but it should be clear is that it *is* time-limited.

There are a number of things related to the ending of interim ministry to consider. If these are ignored, it may make the termination hurtful and perhaps even damaging to the congregation.

Setting the Stage

Setting the stage for termination begins in the initial meetings, before the interim is hired. At some point during the initial discussion with those responsible for hiring, remind them that the established agreement has a clause saying the interim won't be considered for the position of settled pastor. On the first Sunday in the pulpit, make a statement to the effect that the interim isn't going to be the settled pastor. This is also a good time to remind people that you, as the interim, may do things they don't like and they can take heart because the interim won't be here for that long.

As a part of setting the stage, I also point out that some things I say could be blunt or hurtful. I make it clear that it's never my intention to hurt anyone; but because I'm here for a limited time, it may be necessary to be more direct than I would be if there was an unlimited amount of time to build context for saying what I think needs to be said.

Following the initial sermon where I make it clear I'm an interim—fully explaining my role as an Interim, a Transitional, or an Intentional Interim Pastor—I then regularly remind people that I'm temporary. I also begin telling them that when I leave, I won't have contact with the congregation for at least a year, and only after that if the settled pastor invites me. While serving as an interim, it's rare that I have a month go by in which I don't say something about my impermanence or about what will happen when the settled pastor arrives.

Keeping My Word (Integrity)

One of the most important things to do as an interim is to maintain your integrity. A person with integrity will do what they say they'll do and won't flip-flop on important issues. In some instances, an interim may be asked to become settled pastor. Off-hand, I can't think of a single church I've served as an interim where someone didn't ask if I could stay on as pastor. I always have to reaffirm that I won't.

The agreement I sign as an interim for my denomination makes it clear that an interim (at any level) will not be a candidate for settled pastor. There have been instances where I really liked the congregation and wished I could become the settled pastor; but to do that would be a lack of integrity and would also send a message that I couldn't be trusted.

It's important for the interim not to stay on as a settled pastor because the relationship between the interim and the congregation will change. Things never continue as they were when the interim breaks their word.

An interim who wishes to become the settled pastor may say, "God is leading me to be pastor." My response to that is, "Where was God when the original agreement was made?" In effect, that interim is saying God approves of breaking a promise to a congregation. If there's any possibility someone may want to be pastor of a particular congregation, then it's imperative they say no to serving as an interim. Anything else not only displays a lack of integrity on the interim's part, but also implies that God is lacking in integrity.

Saying Goodbye

It would be rare to ever leave a church and not have some people genuinely sad to see you go. (There are probably some who are genuinely *glad* to see you go too!) I personally have never left a church where I didn't genuinely grieve over leaving. However, my goal in leaving is to prepare the congregation for the settled pastor who will follow.

Leading up to my departure, I find it helpful to talk about how to treat a settled pastor. In my final sermon, I try to make the departure a normal part of the process of calling a settled pastor. There are two scriptures I like to use, but I have to say right up front that I'm doing some violence to the passages because I'm taking them out of context and applying them to the termination of an interim.

One passage is from David's final comments to his son Solomon before David's death. In the New International Translation, David says he's going "the way of all the earth." (2 Kings 2:4) I seek to normalize the grief (or perhaps in some cases the joy) of my departure. It isn't a tragedy; it's what I came to do.

The second passage is from John 12:27. Jesus says to his disciples just prior to his betrayal and crucifixion, "For this very reason I came to this hour." Again, the message is an attempt to normalize my departure, a reminder that from the very beginning I was working toward the time when I would leave.

Chapter 8:
Stages of Changing Pastors

IN THE PROCESS OF CHANGING SETTLED PASTORS, there are stages a church goes through. Even though the transitional pastor won't be a direct part of all stages of the process, it doesn't diminish the importance of being aware of what the individual stages have to offer.

Discovering the Coming Change

There are a variety of ways a congregation may learn there will be a change in settled pastors. The news may come as a shock, or the change may have been anticipated. If someone is retiring, everyone will likely know the change has been coming. Still, some people are good at denial and will put the thought out of their mind until it's inescapable.

I remember one church I served where I had been telling the congregation for a couple of months that I was leaving. There was even a church-wide celebration of my ministry. However, on the day of the celebration, a member who was almost always in attendance came to me and said he "wished" he had known I was leaving. He'd been in denial that a change was coming.

A pastor going to another church or changing vocations can be another time the congregation has to deal with a change in pastoral leadership. The change may be totally unexpected or there may have been hints that something was up. There's usually a period of time between the announcement of the ending of the ministry and the time when the pastor is actually gone. This allows for some adjustment to take place.

Nevertheless, there are occasions when a pastor leaves without any warning at all. This can occur in cases where the pastor has suddenly taken ill, is in an accident of some sort, or dies. In these situations, there will be a lot of shock in the congregation, but there will also be a need for immediate action.

A special case is when a pastor has been involved in some sort of ethical or criminal activity. In these cases, there will be a sudden disappearance. A congregation (or part of the congregation) might come to church on a Sunday morning and find no one to deliver a sermon. In some cases, there may also be a legal or ethical constraint over telling anyone why the pastor is gone.

One final case happens when there has been a growing divide between the church and a pastor and they've reached an impasse. In these cases, most congregants will be aware of something happening and they'll have come to their own conclusions. Some will be supportive of the pastor and angry that he is being "forced out." Others may be angry at the pastor, blaming him for whatever has brought the impasse about. There's usually an extended period of time when people know it's likely the pastor will leave, but also an ongoing uncertainty about when it's going to happen.

Working Through the Parting Process

Regardless of the reason for a pastor leaving a congregation, there will be a period of adjustment. There may be a lot of grief at the loss of a spiritual leader. Some people may struggle with feeling elated that the pastor is leaving and then feeling guilty for their reaction.

If there are mixed feelings about a pastor leaving, there might be conflicts within the congregation hidden under the surface. These conflicts can make the departure process harder on everyone involved. A congregation may begin to turn against itself and blame one another.

The congregation will have to work through a lot of feelings surrounding the pastor leaving. It's unlikely those feelings will be resolved in the short run. Perhaps the pastor retiring would be the most likely scenario where the process will be relatively quick to work thorough.

Deciding On Immediate Action Needed

Regardless of the reason for a pastor's leaving a congregation, there will be things that need to be done. In most cases, there will be a need to decide who will fill the pulpit. This means deciding whether to hire an interim or to just go from person to person on Sundays.

The anxiety of the church will be high. Since the pastor may represent the spiritual head of the church, there can be almost a feeling of "lostness" within the church. In the desperation to find a spiritual anchor, a church may turn to someone who doesn't have any deep understanding of what the church is going through.

Selecting a trained Transitional Pastor is new to many congregations. They see the need for filling the pulpit and will see a Transitional Pastor or an Intentional Interim Pastor merely as someone to fill the pulpit. It is at this point the church needs guidance from denominational staff about the difference. Without that, there may be a whole new set of conflicts.

Hiring an Interim Minister: Who Do You Negotiate With?

Unless a church opts for a series of pulpit supplies, at some point there will need to be the decision to hire a Transitional Pastor. A denomination staff person can usually assist a congregation in finding a qualified person. In my denomination, there's a national resource for transitional ministries. Also, the Interim Ministry Network maintains a listing of trained Intentional Interim Pastors.

A trained Transitional Pastor doesn't necessarily need to come from the same denomination as the congregation. Most of their service won't be primarily theological in nature. Having said that, someone from within the same denominational background will already have some understanding of how churches in that denomination usually function. Someone from outside the denomination may have to learn this anew.

There will need to be clear negotiations between the church and the transitional minister. The content of those negations is discussed in Chapter 4 in the section on "Who Do You Negotiate With?" and don't need to be rehashed here. Once the church has decided on and hires a Transitional Pastor, the work begins.

Understanding a Church's Past, Present, and Future

One of the first tasks of the Transitional Pastor is to help the church understand where it's at in this point in history. This involves what has been called the "Five Developmental Points" or the "Five Focus Points." These points are a good way to understand how the church arrived at its current situation, what that current situation is, and what the future may hold for the church. These will be dealt with more fully in a following section. For the sake of a preview, they are:

- ✓ Heritage
- ✓ Leadership
- ✓ Mission/Vision/Identity
- ✓ Connections
- ✓ Future

This area is the focus of my work in transitional ministry. That doesn't mean there won't be other areas in a church that need attention. There may be times when a church is experiencing an unusual level of grief at the loss of a pastor. When that's the case, I spend more time in helping the church work through the grieving process. How that's done partly depends on the situation. In general, I want the church to be aware that God is in charge and that God won't abandon them.

Another area that may need special attention is conflict. If there's major conflict in the church, transforming the conflict into something useful may be the main focus of the interim's work. This is important enough that I included a chapter (*"Conflict as a Part of Transitional Ministries"*) on dealing with conflict.

The ultimate success of the interim period might be measured by how well the "Past, Present, and Future" dimension of the interim period is attended to.

Discovering What Needs to Change

The next dimension of the cycle is discovering what needs to change. I have heard this referred to as what is "broken" and needs repair before the new settled pastor arrives. Generally, I like to focus on what is good in a church; but in this case I like the "broken" language because it has shock value and leads people to consider aspects of their experience in a church that may have been overlooked, repressed, or denied.

I developed a survey to help understand the "broken" areas of a church. I talk more about the survey and include a copy in Appendix B.

One area of the church's functioning that will need special consideration is the amount of time spent on pastoral duties. When I began ministry, there was a bias against any church that didn't have a "full-time" pastor. By the same token, a pastor who wasn't working full-time in a church position was somewhat suspect. All of that has changed.

Today, I find that many churches are struggling to keep their doors open. The decline in church attendees has resulted in fewer people and less income to do the work of the church. A church, in taking a realistic approach to their income, may notice the staff is the largest part of the church budget. Therefore, the quickest way to cut expenses is to cut back on the church staff hours, and that includes cutting back on the hours a pastor is expected to work.

I've heard it said many times that there's "no such thing as a part-time pastor." I agree with that statement because 1) a pastor is seen as a pastor whenever or wherever they're known, and 2) the work comes at hours which make it very hard not to be on call, in some way, twenty-four hours a day. Whenever I'm working as a transitional pastor doing less than full-time equivalent service, I still receive emails and phone calls during hours I'm supposedly not working. What's being communicated to me is important and I wouldn't want people to *not* communicate, but it means that my other endeavors are often interrupted.

To reflect the reality that there isn't really such a thing as a part-time pastor, the term "bi-vocational pastor" has come into common use. That's a reflection of the fact the person has two vocations—two jobs—both of which will have demands on the pastor's time, talents, and physical and mental resources.

Part of the Transitional Pastor's job is to be sure the church understands the implications of deciding to go "bi-vocational" as opposed to "full-time." The primary benefit is that the church should be better able to compensate a bi-vocational pastor because the compensation is less likely to include things like health insurance or retirement benefits. Depending on the pastor's second vocational choice, a second benefit may be that the pastor will have connections with another part of the community that wouldn't otherwise be available.

The disadvantages are, as they've been mentioned before: limitations on the pastor's time devoted to the church. Too much demand can lead to burnout or to outright mental health issues, such as depression, anxiety, and repressed hostility. In addition, a pastor attempting to meet the needs of both vocations may end up ignoring or short-changing family and spouse relations.

The decision to put these burdens on a pastor is best explored by a church before putting a settled pastor into a bi-vocational position.

Going to a bi-vocational ministry puts an extra burden on the church to care for and protect the pastor from the disadvantages. I want to make clear to the church that it is their responsibility. To say they expect the bi-vocational pastor to protect their own boundaries isn't realistic.

Another common tactic is for a church to specifically look for a pastor who has a spouse who works and has benefits like health insurance. This means the pastor can be full-time without costing the church so much money. That can be helpful as far as the church's budget is concerned. However, the church needs to understand they're taking advantage of the spouse for the sake of the church. Part of me wonders about the church ethics of intentionally taking that course of action without acknowledging the full impact of what they are doing. A question to consider is: If the spouse loses healthcare coverage, will the church pick that up for the pastor and their family?

I should add: that mindset has long been a part of the church's approach to compensating someone for the work of ministry. In my ministry, there were many times when we as a family couldn't have made ends meet without my wife's income. I know I'm not a unique case.

All of this is important for a church to be aware of if they're deciding to change the amount of time for which they're able to compensate a pastor. It will save some conflict and hurt feelings at later date if these issues are understood from the beginning.

Implementing Changes that Are Possible

Once the church as a whole has discovered things that need to be changed, the Transitional Pastor can help the church decide what can realistically be changed and what will need to be acknowledged as needing change even though it may not be currently possible. In the negotiating process, it's important to honestly inform a potential settled pastor of the issues needing "repair." To not do so is to hire someone under false pretenses.

A common complaint of newly settled pastors is that the church didn't really give them an accurate picture of the situation they were stepping into. I've heard congregational leaders acknowledge they were being less than candid for fear the candidate might not consider accepting the position if they understood the full situation. To not be honest is to set the stage for a short pastorate and major conflicts in a congregation.

It's a daunting task for a church to look at what needs to change before the arrival of a new settled pastor and determine what can wait until later. There are many things to consider, such as money, personnel available, how long the changes will take to be accomplished, and how the changes will affect the church in the long run. Some churches avoid making changes because the task is so daunting, assuming things will be easier when there's a settled pastor. That usually isn't true. The new pastor carries a burden that should have been shared by the whole congregation.

The transitional minister—whether an Interim Pastor, Transitional Pastor, Intentional Interim Pastor, or even just an Ongoing Pulpit Supply—should keep in mind that the congregation must decide what changes will need to be made. Those who have been in this form of ministry will be aware of changes that could, and possibly should, be made. Still, deciding to make the changes and actually implementing changes is up to the congregation. The interim may point out areas where change would be helpful, but that is different from insisting the church make the changes or "shaming" the church if the changes aren't made.

This is an ego issue for the interim. The more the interim's ego gets involved, the more likely they will insist on specific changes. The interim isn't the settled pastor and won't be. Insistence on changes that suit the interim may result in more difficulties for the settled pastor.

The nature of the changes that need to be made will be different from one congregation to another. There are things that are somewhat common across congregations. However, the exact changes within a particular congregation will vary. Look for needed changes in bi-laws, policy and procedures, the lay leadership of the church, the mission or identity of the church, and budgeting issues. If changes are needed in any of these areas, or other areas, call attention to them. If the church rejects the suggestions, it may be helpful to point out specific problems that may arise (note the problems *may* arise, not *will* arise—every church is different). No matter what a congregation decides, it's helpful to bless them for taking a stand for what they believe to be the direction God is leading them.

Doing the Search Process
(Activating the Search Committee)

This stage of the cycle is often set forth in a congregation's by-laws. It's often the congregation's first goal as soon as the previous pastor has left, sometimes as soon as the previous pastor resigns. Despite the urgency the congregation may feel, it's helpful to slow down the process so the church has time to understand who they are before they begin searching.

Denominational judicatories will each have their guidelines for how to go about the search process. Some of these guidelines have been carefully thought out and constantly revised to keep pace with our changing society. However, some of the guidelines are "common sense" and may be less than helpful.

It's important for the interim to understand the denominational guidelines and procedures, as well as the individual congregation's guidelines and procedures so as not to work in opposition to them.

I believe one very helpful aspect of a trained interim ministry is that it gives the search committee someone they can go to who isn't a part of the congregation or part of the candidate pool. This is part of the reason why I believe it's so important for an interim minster to make it clear they aren't a candidate for the position of settled pastor. A search committee needs a neutral source of information.

Interviewing Candidates
and Narrowing the Selection

When selection of potential candidates and the interview process begins, the interim should stay clear. It's not the job of the interim to influence the selection or interview process one way or another. A congregation may choose someone who the interim doesn't approve of. Staying out of the way can be difficult for the interim, but is essential.

There's one way the interim can be useful in the selection and interview process: The transitional minister can be available for a "mock interview." This gives the committee a chance to ask questions, see which questions help, and which are less helpful. When the "real" interview comes up, the members of the committee will be less anxious.

Negotiations with the New Settled Pastor

This is basically a hands-off part of the process for the interim. It's hard not to get into the position of negotiating on behalf of the incoming pastor. The only thing the transitional minister can do that might be helpful is to check with the committee before they begin negotiations to see if they've left anything important out of the negotiation process.

Formal Call of a New Settled Pastor

Calling a settled pastor is totally in the congregation's purview.

Termination of the Interim Relationship

A church may not know how to end a relationship with a pastor well. That may be because there was conflict with a former pastor. The termination of the interim ministry period may be an opportunity to help the church discover what's helpful in ending a ministry relationship.

A review of the transitional process is helpful to the church as well as to the transitional minister. In most cases, the church will be focused on the incoming settled pastor and if a review is to happen the transitional pastor will have to initiate it. This is a chance to find out what worked well and what could be improved in the next transitional ministry position.

Keep in mind that how you as the interim react will set the stage for the incoming settled pastor.

Beginning Again

This is all in the purview of the church and the new settled pastor.

Installation of a New Settled Pastor

This is all in the purview of the church and the new settled pastor.

The process between the ending of one settled pastorate and the beginning of a new one isn't always linear and will vary from congregation to congregation.

Chapter 9:
Process Tasks of the Interim Minister

Everything is a process. There are stages everything has to go through. Sometimes the stages happen in rapid succession, at other times things are drawn out. When you're aware of the process, it makes it easier to move through each stage. A lack of awareness can result in wasted time or in one being at the mercy of the process with little control.

Every transitional pastor goes through a step-by-step process with a congregation. This is different than the process the congregation will go through (as was previously discussed). The effectiveness of the interim process will in part depend on the interim's awareness of what is happening.

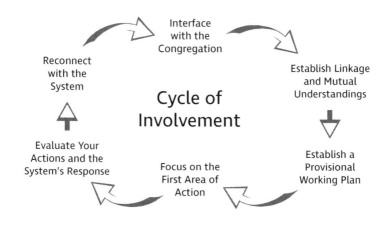

Reconnect
with the
System

Interface
with the
Congregation

Establish Linkage
and Mutual
Understandings

**Cycle of
Involvement**

Evaluate Your
Actions and the
System's Response

Focus on the
First Area of
Action

Establish a
Provisional
Working Plan

Interface with the Congregation

Perhaps the most difficult thing a transitional pastor has to do is to walk through the door for the first time. Everything they say or do, every judgment[5] they make about the congregation will impact the rest of their interim ministry with the congregation. Ideally, the interim would withhold all judgments, but the reality is that we *will* make assessments about a congregation, and the best any of us can do is to remind ourselves that those judgments are provisional.

Every church is in some way a system. A system is a set of interconnecting parts that work together for some purpose. The transitional pastor will have to come to grips with how the system works or how it is dysfunctional.

Encountering a system means coming to an opinion about the system and what's happening within that system. In some ways, forming opinions about a congregation starts before we even meet people in that system. Those opinions will be influenced by what we know of the congregation, the size of the congregation, and—if the former settled pastor is known personally—the previous pastoral leadership of the congregation. Basically, any information, valid or invalid, will affect the opinions formed. It's important to keep in mind that those opinions may not truly reflect who the congregation is and those opinions may need to be altered.

The flip side of encountering a system is that the system itself will be forming an opinion about the transitional pastor. That also will have started as soon as the church hears the transitional minister's name. If someone recommended the transitional minister for a particular interim position, then the congregation's opinion of

---

5   I'm using the word judgment to mean "an opinion." The way I'm using it doesn't include a moral value of "good" or "bad."

that person (among other things) will, in turn, affect their opinion of the transitional minister.

Establish Linkage and Mutual Understandings

Once you have encountered the system, you have to find a way to connect with the system. You cannot do ministry and remain disconnected from those you are ministering to. It's to the *system* one is connecting, not to individuals. Individuals are a part of the system. A congregational system is a complex interrelationship of experiences, understandings, and hopes.

You might connect with a system by connecting with individuals, but that isn't to be assumed. There's no way to be sure in the early stages of an interim ministry the nature of an individual's relationship with the system. A system may see specific individuals as "outside the system." If that is so, the transitional pastor may be working with a congregation but not really encounter the system because they are kept at a distance.

I don't know of any church that exists outside of connections with other groups. They may be community groups, faith groups (such as ministerial associations), or denominational groups. You'll want to consider how you'll connect with these groups, too, and the impact it will have on the church system you're primarily involved with.

Based On How the Congregation Functions, Establish a Provisional Working Plan

A necessary step in this process is assessing how the system works. Otherwise, you may end up connected with the system and simply be carried along without understanding what's actually happening. It's important to know why things happen the way they do within a particular system. From that information, you can make tentative judgments about what effect changes will have.

Focus On the First Area of Action

The transitional pastor will have to decide where the first area of action needs to be taken. This is about deciding on a point that will be the focus of your ministry. Because a system is a dynamic entity, what the focus is at one point won't necessarily be the focus at another point. To say "the first area of action" is misleading because it is actually the "current area of action."

Evaluate Your Actions and the System's Response

Constant evaluation of what's happening in the system is important. The evaluation includes how you feel about the process and how others feel about the process. Always look at what you're doing with the understanding that it may be the perfect thing that needed to be done or... it may be the absolutely worst thing that could have been done. Which way your actions lean depends in part on your beliefs about what's happening.

The system will also respond to what is happening. It is important to listen to the system's response. Avoid judgments (in the sense of something being good or bad) about the intentions of the system.

A system can be very supportive of the transitional pastor for a number of reasons. It may be that the church's system really believes in you and wants you to succeed—they see that as being in their own best interests. On the other hand, a system may appear to be very supportive because the congregation assumes that will "keep you off their backs." They may have learned how to deflect leadership by seeming to support the leadership and then going on to do whatever they've always done.

The Cycle

Once you've gone through encountering the system, connecting with the system, assessing the system, and assessing your and the church's reactions to the system, it will be necessary to start again. Everything you do will change the system in one way or another. If you're uncomfortable with fluidity, you will have a hard time as a Transitional Pastor or as an Intentional Interim Pastor.

Also be aware that you may be taking more than one action at a time. That means each action will be affecting the system individually and that the interaction between multiple actions will also affect the system.

Summary

The job of transitional pastor is often thought of as an easy alternative when a pastor has left settled ministry. I believe the job of a transitional pastor is actually more complicated than that of a settled pastor. One reason for that is a transitional pastor will have to do all the things a settled pastor does while also keeping a close eye on where the church is going. Your impact on the church is urgent. You'll only be there for a few months. It's important to not assume you'll accomplish everything you set out to do.

Chapter 10:
Five Focus Points for a Church

IN TRAINING FOR INTENTIONAL INTERIM MINISTRY, there are five things singled out for a church to consider in preparing to call a new settled pastor. These "Focus Points" facilitate a church's understanding of itself before they call a pastor. Another term for the Focus Points is "Developmental Tasks." This term has fallen out of use because it implies every church is the same and that there's a particular set of things that have to happen in sequence.

> "A developmental task is a task that arises at or about a certain period in life, unsuccessful achievement of which leads to inability to perform tasks associated with the next period or stage in life."[6]

This is a definition that directly applies to human developmental tasks. At different stages in life, different tasks must be accomplished if there's to be progress in one's life. At one time, these tasks were seen as linear, with one task following another and with each task being complete before the next task can begin. We now recognize that the world and human development isn't neatly packaged with a bow on top.

Five Focus Points (Developmental Tasks) have been identified for churches that are between pastors. These Focus Points will vary in terms of their relative importance, but each plays a significant

---

6   www.wvdhhr.org/bph/modules/man/man-res3.htm

part in a church understanding who it is before calling a settled pastor. Many churches struggle with finding a new pastor who is a good fit for them because they haven't focused on these points.

In addition to the Five Focus Points, there is one thing that does fit the definition of "developmental task." That's the process of grieving and obtaining some degree of closure. Some churches and former pastors do well with closure. Others don't deal with closure issues at all. Because the former pastor is no longer on the scene, it may be assumed that "closure" has automatically been accomplished. Closure can be a long process that continues into the interim period and perhaps into the time of the next settled pastor as well.

After considering issues related to closure and grief, your attention should be turned to the Five Focus Points (Five Developmental Tasks). While they're presented as discrete, individual processes in this section, in reality they won't be that clearly differentiated within a congregation. As previously indicated, they will usually overlap.

The Five Focus Points are presented in a logical order, but depending on the situation of a particular congregation, the order may change. There's no one "correct" order for the Focus Points to be presented to a congregation.

Focus Point - Heritage

A church needs to know its heritage, but the term "heritage" can lend itself to misunderstanding. It isn't just about the history of the church. The history of a church is a part of its heritage, but only one part. Heritage is about the influences from history that are carried on in the present. One way of saying this is that "history" is about what has happened in the past. "Heritage" is about how those past events influence the present."

It's almost always easier to talk about heritage as the good things that have been passed on. It may have been overcoming a financial crisis, a period of church growth, or some event enjoyed by the church. These are readily accepted as a part of a church's heritage. These successes aren't usually hard to identify. A congregation may brag about them.

However, heritage isn't what specific successes were, but how those success affect the church in the present. Does the church have a particular mindset because it was successful in some ministry or in the face of a crisis?

In addition to positive things, there are also negative and hurtful events that result in attitudes that affect how a church behaves. These are often dismissed as "history." It's an attempt to deny something really happened, or to deny that the issue has any relevance for the current time. Sometimes negative events in a congregation's history are covered up in an attempt to deny they really happened. A church may have had a split, or a pastor may have had an affair or absconded with church funds. These events can determine how a congregation will respond to any number of events in the future, not just the exact same situation.

Negative events are a part of the heritage of a congregation. For instance, a church split over some point of theology may result in hesitance to deal with any issue where there's a difference of opinion, regardless of whether or not it's a theological difference. In addition, the points of view and attitudes developed as a result of the negative event can continue on for decades, even into multiple generations.

Denying those things often results in attitudes that don't make sense to people who weren't, directly or indirectly, a part of the original event. Perhaps a purely fictitious example will help. Imagine a former pastor ran off with the red-headed church secretary. This event happened forty years ago and only a few of those who were adults and understood what happened are still around today. The current pastor is hiring a new secretary and she happens to be red-headed. From within the church there's strong opposition to hiring that particular woman. The opposition may be triggered by the color of her hair and nothing else. A part of the heritage of the church is that red hair means potential problems with the pastor.

The reverse may also be true. A former red-headed secretary may have been unusually skillful and employed when the church was growing. Now there's resistance to hiring any secretary other than a red-head. Again, the hair color is irrelevant other than it calls to mind, probably unconsciously, a past history. It's believed at some level that a red-headed secretary will be a benefit to the church.

It's important for a church to know its heritage, both positive heritage and negative heritage. Of course, getting the congregation to recognize its positive or negative heritage is easier said than done.

There are a variety of ways to bring potential heritage issues to light. One may ask directly: What are positive events in the church's history that affect what's happening here today? It can also be asked what negative events still affect how the church responds to current situations. When you ask these two questions informally, it gives you a reference point when a church makes surprising decisions or exhibits unexpected resistance. It may help to bring up these events and ask how they might be affecting current attitudes.

A congregation's heritage isn't as simple as identifying one solitary event that has affected attitudes. It's more often the case that something happened repeatedly to shape the attitudes of a church in the present. It's helpful if a transitional pastor looks for repeated events and asks how those events are still influencing the church. This is true of both positive and negative events.

Churches are more likely to talk about positive events that shape attitudes than negative events. It's a natural human tendency to want to deny the ugly parts of history. The survey in Appendix B is, in part, an attempt to get at some of those negative things.

Focus Point - Mission/Vision/Identity

The terminology around what constitutes a mission statement and a vision for a congregation varies from denomination to denomination and even within a single denomination. In some cases, what I refer to with the words "mission" and "vision" is referred to as a church's "identity."

Sometimes there's a distinction made between what a "mission statement" is and what a "vision statement" is. The labels are secondary. A congregation does need to know why it's there and what it's supposed to be doing. I believe the actual identity of a church is defined by the interaction of all five of the Focus Points. However, it's important to be able to state that mission/vision/ identity in a concise manner.

A mission/vision/identity statement says why the church exists. More specifically, why this particular church exists where it does and what it does in that location. Mission/vision statements come and go. In searching for a pastor, a congregation needs some idea of where it's going at that moment in time. The mission/vision/identity statement is a simple way for a congregation to say why it believes it exists and what it's going to do about existing where it does.

A church is wise to revisit or even rewrite their mission statement during the interim. At the same time, the church needs to remember that a new pastor may want to revisit this process as well. A mission/vision/identity statement has a shelf-life of about five years. In that time, hopefully a church will have grown spiritually and will see different aspects of what they're doing compared to what they saw when the statement was written.

The transitional pastor should minimize their influence on the mission/vision/identity statement. The transitional pastor must keep in mind that the interim position is temporary and the goal is to prepare the church for the next settled pastor.

There is one thing related to a vision statement churches need to be cautious about: Sometimes in the interview process a church will ask what the potential pastor's vision is for the church. That's a very poor question. Unless a candidate has had a long involvement with the church, whatever vision they have of the church will be somewhat unrealistic. How can a person have a realistic vision if the congregation is still largely unknown?

What tends to happen is the candidate will give a very general reply that would work with any congregation in any setting. It will sound good because it fits a very generalized picture of what any congregation might be hoping for. But when the vision doesn't match what the congregation, consciously or unconsciously, wants, both the pastor and the congregation will be disappointed.

Another issue with mission/vision/identity statements is that congregations can get wrapped up in wanting to "sound" spiritual. It may become imperative that the word "Jesus" or "God" or "Christ" appears as a part of the statement. Without those specific terms the statement may not "sound" spiritual enough to some; but the very purpose of the mission/vision/identity statement is to express the church's understanding of why God has brought them together in that time and place.

Another pitfall of mission/vision/identity statements is that a congregation may try to include everything possible in the statement. Some mission/vision/identity statements can be so long that, by the time you get to the end, you've forgotten what was said at the beginning. The statement needs to be concise and cover the most important reason for the church's existence. It also needs to be specific enough that it will differentiate that particular congregation from other congregations.

It also helps to make a distinction between a "motto" and a "mission/vision/identity statement." A motto is short and describes some characteristic of the congregation. That characteristic may or may not have an active component. "We are a friendly church" or "We are a welcoming church" may be acceptable mottos, but don't really make a statement about the church's mission or identity. There would need to be something about how the church is welcoming and what the result of being a welcoming congregation will be in terms of their God-given mission.

A question for a congregation to ask about their mission/vision/ identity statement is: "Will someone who's a stranger understand the purpose of the church from this statement?" Does the statement make it clear to someone who's new to the congregation what they're getting themselves into if they join that church?

A mission/vision/identity statement should be useful for determining what ministries will be attempted by a church. If a new ministry is proposed in the church, the mission/vision/identity statement can be used to see if it's really a ministry that's in line with that congregation's understanding of what God expects of them.

Focus Point - Leadership

A church needs to look at their leadership issues before calling a new pastor. There are two aspects to leadership: "How does the church understand pastoral leadership?" and, just as important, "How does a church understand lay leadership?"

There are different styles of pastoral leadership. Some pastoral leaders will be laid back and wait for the congregation (or smaller group) to decide where it wants to go, then they'll step up to give leadership in that direction. Other pastoral leaders will be filled to the brim with ideas and immediately try to get people to accept their ideas.

Some pastoral leaders will be collaborative in their approach. Their goal will be to get everyone involved in making decisions. For those who want to collaborate, working with others is the most important part of pastoral leadership.

Some pastoral leaders may be more dominate. These pastoral leaders may take charge and work hard to get their ideas accepted. They may get those ideas from their own study and prayer, or as a part of a collaborative process with the congregational leaders or the congregation as a whole.

Some pastoral leaders will be *laissez-faire*. Their expectation is that needed changes will occur naturally. They see no need for them to push anything and may even see pushing a particular agenda as harmful to the church.

Some pastoral leaders are just the opposite of *laissez-faire*. When they come into a congregation, they will want to make changes immediately. Their goal is to shake things up so growth will occur.

Keep in mind there's no one right style of leadership. The style will depend on the person's background and how they've developed as a human being. Congregations will respond positively to one type of leadership style and will respond negativity to another. What style works depends on the individual congregation.

It's important to look at this Focus Point because, if a church has no awareness of what style works for it, they may end up with a pastor whose style rubs them the wrong way. There's a high probability they'll be looking for another pastor in a relatively short time.

The transitional pastor can't dictate what style of pastor the church will work best with. This can be difficult because, if the interim is an experienced transitional pastor, they'll begin to spot what styles of pastoral leadership will probably work best in particular congregations. The danger for the interim is that they'll assume they have the "final" answer and unconsciously push for a certain style.

To avoid this, the transitional pastor needs a clear understanding of their own identity and the style of leadership they bring to the church. I would also warn: Simply because a church responds to a particular style of interim leadership doesn't mean they'd respond as well to that same style of leadership in a settled pastor. What the interim should do is bring the idea of leadership styles to the forefront of the congregation's consciousness so the congregation can make an informed decision.

The other element of leadership to be considered is lay leadership. *How* the congregation chooses its lay leaders is important for them to understand, along with the advantages and disadvantages of choosing the way that they do.

I've discovered that many churches subscribe to the "who will do it" theory of selecting leadership. This is particularly true of small churches with a limited pool of potential leaders. They see a job that needs to be done and they will select whoever wants to do the job. The lay leader's qualifications and skills are often a very low priority in the selection process.

A helpful approach is for the transitional pastor to talk about leadership with the whole church and to hold trainings on leadership with smaller groups. The interim can take risks in talking about leadership that a settled pastor might be more reticent (with good reason) to take.

Related to leadership, there may need to be a review of the governance documents of the church. The church's constitution or by-laws are often left unchallenged for many years and were developed for a congregation that has changed dramatically.

In the recent years, there have been big changes in the ways a church might conduct business. Almost all of the by-laws I've read assume that people will be able to be physically present when conducting business. With the Covid-19 crisis, it became evident that there needs to be a way of conducting business remotely or by means of email or ground mail.

A church I served during the crisis is an example of this issue. The by-laws called for the church council to select the search committee and then the selection would be affirmed by a church vote. Under normal circumstances, there would be no problem with getting the church approval. A business meeting following morning worship would be called. Then the church would vote to either approve or not approve the selection.

With the stay-at-home orders in place, the church couldn't announce the meeting and, if it did, it couldn't gather to hold the meeting. The by-laws/constitution had no provisions for email or mail-in ballots or for electronic voting through Zoom or some other platform. As a result, the whole process was on hold until the stay-at-home orders were withdrawn or until a creative interpretation of the by-laws could be arrived at.

Even though it will be highly unlikely that any set of by-laws will cover all possible situations, it is possible to be flexible enough to cover many situations. A transitional pastor may be able help a church understand the possible problems and solutions to those potential problems.

Focus Point - Connections

"Connections" covers a wide range of ways other entities and the church are connected. I've seen this interpreted narrowly, referring only to the church's connection to a particular denomination. Although very important, that's a much too narrow view for our purposes.

It's important for a church to know, outside of its denominational connections, what other churches it's connected to. There are any number of things different churches might do together. There are times when churches from different denominations come together for ministry, like Vacation Bible School. Some churches share parking lots, alternating the time each service starts to maximize the availability of parking. And some of these connections are semi-formal, such as when churches connect thorough another legal entity like a food bank. There are also chaplaincy programs that are undertaken in cooperation with other churches.

All of these things need to be in the awareness of a church before they begin the search process. If a church has a close relationship with another church in a different denomination, they'll have problems if they call a pastor who's only willing to work with churches from their own denomination.

Another aspect of connections which can sometimes be overlooked is: How do members of the church relate to other secular organizations in the community? For instance, are some church members teachers (relationship with the school system), police officers (relationships with the law enforcement community), or doctors or nurses (relationships with the medical community)? The list of possible connections is endless.

The connection to the denomination is important for churches that are denominational. However, that connection may be multi-faceted. In American Baptist Churches, there are connections with the national body and also connections with a city or regional body. What's more, within the regional connection there may be associational connections. Churches need to be aware of those ties.

Often a church won't realize how connected they are with a national or regional body. I know of one occasion where a church decided its connections weren't very important and called a pastor with no previous denominational connections. That pastor then took the church *out* of the denominational connections. Later the church needed help and went to the region asking for help, and they were surprised when the region couldn't help because they were on longer affiliated with that region.

Focus Point - Future

The last of the Five Focus Points is "future." I think it's a human tendency to proceed in life with the assumption that what's going to happen is the same as what's been happening all along. That's true for congregations as well as individuals.

A church needs to have some general idea of the future (I say "general idea" because the exact nature of the future is always hidden from us). Without a consideration of the church's future in terms of the community the church is in and the forces that are affecting the church—whether those forces be from around the state, the nation, or even the world—the result in terms of a settled pastor will be less than satisfying.

I've run across churches who decided they didn't need to think too much about what the church was like because it hadn't been all that long since they called their previous pastor. They thought all they needed to do was a quick update to the church profile. The erroneousness of that idea is most clearly illuminated by the Covid-19 virus. In a period of a couple of months, perhaps only a couple of weeks, the world changed irrevocably. Some churches were able to adapt to the situation and make changes, others sought to keep things the same as they were before the crisis, and still others learned they weren't prepared for the adaptions needed and discovered how to become more flexible.

There are three future-oriented questions that need to be addressed by the church as a whole:

1. "What are the trends in their community?"
2. "What are the trends in the congregation?"
3. "What does the church need in a pastor to address the issues those trends might present?"

The trends in the community relate to changing demographics. Is the community the church is going to minister to growing older or younger, becoming ethnically diverse or ethnically homogeneous, becoming more economically affluent or economically depressed? All these, and other factors, will affect what traits the church needs in a pastor.

The future of the church also will depend on who's a part of the congregation. The same three questions asked about the community can also be applied to the church. Taking only one of the comparisons above as an example: Is the giving-base of the church increasing or decreasing in economic affluence? What characteristics of a pastor will best serve the congregation as it looks into the future? These are important questions to ask when searching for a settled pastor.

Determining the characteristics of a new settled pastor is always a difficult task. I've seen churches who call a pastor using the same criteria they used to call the last pastor. The new pastor looked great and the congregation was excited to get things going again.

However, the new pastor was called to a church that no longer existed because time and experience had already changed it. In a situation like that, a new pastor may arrive only to find they don't meet the present and future needs of the church.

The world is always changing around us and the exact nature of the future is unknown. Still, there are things we can look at to give us clues about what may happen. The congregation as a whole needs to understand the possible future of the church and their community and how that affects calling a new settled pastor. Otherwise the search committee may find resistance to their process.

It's a wise church that considers the potential changes in the community and the congregation as well as potential changes in the way the church performs its ministry. There may be changes on the horizon that will affect income and what programs are viable. There may be a need for changes in the facilities. Not all pastors have the same skills. It is important to call someone who has the right skills for the current job.

Chapter 11:
Working With
the Search Committee and
the Transition Team

THERE ARE SOME ISSUES FOR THE Transitional Pastor which don't fit easily in any one category. Two of these have to do with the Transitional Pastor's work with the search committee, and the other has to do with what the church can do to help the new settled pastor get off to a running start. In some ways the issues are peripheral to the actual work of the Transitional Pastor, and both of these issues are areas where the Transitional Pastor needs to tread carefully.

Perhaps one of the more difficult tasks for any interim pastor is understanding that they aren't going to be the settled pastor. I find it important to keep that in the forefront. If the interim sets up programs or events that suit their work and which are not suited to the incoming settled pastor, it's a disservice to the incoming pastor and the church.

Of course, it isn't possible to work with a congregation for a significant length of time and not influence the programing of the church. There will be necessary procedures and programs set in place as part of the transition process. The question is how to move forward without those things becoming part of the expectation of the church. This is a particularly delicate matter when working with a search committee.

The Transitional Pastor and the Pastoral Search Committee

Often, a pastoral search committee will be made up of individuals with varying degrees of expertise. Some may have served on previous search committees, some may have been involved in searches for personnel in their business life, and still others may be rookies to the whole process. Regardless, the Transitional Pastor may provide help for the committee if the committee is willing to accept the help.

It's important to respect the pastoral search committee's wish (or lack thereof) for the Transitional Pastor's help. There are many different reasons why a pastoral search committee may be hesitant to work with the Transitional Pastor. I've seen pastoral search committees who wanted to be separate from the Transitional Pastor due to a general distrust of the transitional ministry process. If the church had a bad experience with a former interim pastor, it's natural they would be hesitant to work with a new one. Another reason could be that the pastoral search committee believes everything should be kept confidential and that talking to the Transitional Pastor would be a violation of that confidentiality. If that's the case, obviously there are also issues of trust involved. These trust issues may or may not spill over into other areas of the Transitional Pastor's work. The Transitional Pastor should keep these issues in mind and not take the committee's hesitance to work with them as something personal.

Occasionally you may come across a pastoral search committee made up of individuals (or dominated by one or two individuals) who think they know all there is to know about the process. They may take any suggestions from the Transitional Pastor as attacks on their personal competence. There may well be other issues that result in a search committee being hesitant to work closely with a Transitional Pastor. The most the Transitional Pastor can do is make the offer of working with the committee and then trust the congregational process. It's very unlikely that a Transitional Pastor will effect any change in the search committee's attitude in the short time the Transitional Pastor is a part of the congregation.

If the pastoral search committee is open to working with the Transitional Pastor, there are several approaches that can be helpful to the process. There are also some dangers that must be avoided.

The Church Profile and the Transitional Pastor

The Transitional Pastor may be aware of areas of church life that the pastoral search committee overlooks as it prepares a church profile. The Transitional Pastor will be looking at the church with "new eyes" and may see things that the church itself is blind to because of long exposure.

The Transitional Pastor may also help the pastoral search committee by reviewing the church profile that will be sent to potential candidates. It's normal for people to want to put themselves in the best light, and that means a profile might be overly optimistic about the church. If a candidate accepts an interview (or worse yet, the call to be the settled pastor), based on an overly-optimistic church profile, the interview might be difficult when the candidate asks questions the pastoral search committee has no way of answering. It could mean the loss of a potentially great candidate from the search process.

If a pastor accepts the an overly-optimistic church profile as the way things are, then the pastorate may be short lived. It will most likely be filled with tension when the new settled pastor attempts to lead the church in ways that are indicated on the church profile, but which are not reality.

On the flip side, church profiles can also be overly pessimistic. If that's the case, good candidates may not even consider speaking with the pastoral search committee.

Another potential problem is the church profile may be just plain boring. A pastoral search committee may follow what they consider to be the proper format for the profile, but forget the profile needs to stand out. A potential candidate should look at the church profile and say, "This looks interesting!"

The Transitional Pastor must be very self-aware when reviewing a profile. There may be things the Transitional Pastor hopes for the church that won't be included in the profile. The profile doesn't have to please the Transitional Pastor and the Transitional Pastor shouldn't try to make the profile into something they personally approve of.

The review of the profile is best done in order to ensure a clear, accurate, and engaging picture of what the church is like is given to the candidates. In the end, what the profile looks like is up to the pastoral search committee.

The Transitional Pastor and the Mock Interview

A pastoral search committee will at some point need to interview candidates. Sometimes the church will be lucky and have someone who is trained in interviewing job applicants as a part of the search committee. (The "candidate" is considered a job applicant.) At other times (the majority of cases in my experience) the pastoral search committee will not have experience in interviewing job applicants.

There's a difference between hiring a person who must interact with other people as part of the job and hiring someone for tasks not requiring interaction with others. The search committee must be able to discern whether or not a candidate will be the right fit for the job. The Transitional Pastor can set up a mock interview that gives the search committee some experience at asking the right questions and looking beyond basic answers.

It will be important for the Transitional Pastor to keep in mind that their responses, while being honest, must not influence the committee to look for a particular type of candidate. It's easy for the Transitional Pastor's personal orientation to slip into the process and affect how the search committee sees candidates. If the Transitional Pastor has strong feelings about the type of candidate the church should be looking for, then it's probably best not to do a mock interview or to interact with the pastoral search committee at all.

The Pastoral Search Committee and Ongoing Encouragement

There's a good possibility that the search will be frustrating and the pastoral search committee will get discouraged. If the Transitional Pastor has a good working relationship with the pastoral search committee, then they can be a source of strength and hope during the times of discouragement.

I again caution the Transitional Pastor to be aware of the difference between encouraging the search committee and trying to direct them. If a pastoral search committee has a difficult time, it can be tempting to step in and tell them what they need to do or what kind of pastor they need. A hands-off approach is best.

The Transitional Pastor and Questions from the Pastoral Search Committee.

When a pastoral search committee is navigating uncharted waters, they'll have questions they hope the Transitional Pastor can help with. As a general rule, it's not appropriate to answer questions about any candidate. This is something that should be made clear from the beginning. If the candidate is known personally to the Transitional Pastor, it's acceptable to acknowledge that connection, but not to indicate the level of connection or whether the Transitional Pastor thinks the candidate would or would not make a good candidate. In a similar way, it's not appropriate to comment on where the candidate went to school or what the candidate's theological stance is. If the type of school attended or the theological stance is important, the pastoral search committee should do their own research.

The type of questions I will answer are procedural questions. If it's a denominational procedure, I can give general answers. If it's a congregational procedure, I refer the pastoral search committee to the church's by-laws and will seek to help them clarify areas that aren't clear.

One other thing that's important: When the candidate is brought to the congregation, the by-laws must be followed. There's usually a requirement for advance notice a specified number of weeks prior to the candidate coming to preach. There's also usually a business meeting required to extend a call or not extend a call.

The Transitional Pastor, as someone outside the system, is in a good position to monitor procedures to be sure the by-laws are being adhered to.

There may also be questions about what to do on a candidate weekend. That's an acceptable topic for discussion with the Transitional Pastor. It's important the pastoral search committee stay aware of denominational expectations, the candidate's expectations, as well as good hospitality.

Helping the Church Get the New Settled Pastor Off to a Good Start

Another area of concern that is vital—but potentially dangerous—for a Transitional Pastor is advising the church on how to react to the incoming pastor. Whoever the incoming settled pastor may be, they'll be different from the Transitional Pastor. Caution should be exercised in deciding what to suggest and what not to suggest to the church about the relationship they'll have with the new settled pastor. Having provided that caution, there are some steps the Transitional Pastor can take to make things easier for the incoming settled pastor.

At the risk of repeating myself too many times, the first thing the Transitional Pastor can do is make it clear their relationship with the church will end once the transition time is over. That means they won't perform any weddings, funerals, baptisms, or other rites of the church. This can be particularly difficult during the first months of the settled pastor being on the field. The Transitional Pastor will be better known and people may want to use them because of the relationship developed during the transitional period. Each request will have to be considered carefully, on a case-by-case basis. Whatever the circumstances, the settled pastor must have the final say and that must be clearly understood.

Beyond the first two or three months, there can be no excuse for returning to the church. For one thing, the rites of the church are *church* functions. The primacy of the church has the potential to be confused if a particular personality is the main reason for deciding who conducts a service. If a former pastor is brought in to conduct or even participate in a service, it can result in confusion about who the actual pastor of the congregation is. Establishing one's credentials as the leader of a congregation requires that everyone understand what the role of the settled pastor will be.

My last Sunday in a transitional setting, I make it clear I'm not available for any service of the church and that I will separate myself from the congregation. I won't even attend services, and if I'm in contact with someone from the church for some reason, I avoid any discussion of how things are going in the church.

I also ask the people in the congregation to no longer refer to me as "pastor." I ask instead that they call me by my first name. "Pastor" is a term that applies to a particular office, pastor of a particular church. If there's a need for formal introductions, the honorific "reverend" can be used as a recognition of a calling by God to a lifetime of service in a variety of settings.

I also remind the church that the incoming pastor will be different from me as transitional pastor. They can and should be prepared for changes in worship and church functioning.

I also want the church to be aware that they're hiring the pastor and not the pastor's family. That is true except in some cases where a couple might share the role of pastor. In that case, both should be getting paid. However, children are a different matter. One shouldn't expect the children of the pastor to behave in a way different from other children in the church that are their age. A two- or three-year-old child will only understand the church as the place where "Daddy" or Mommy" works, and will be very relaxed in how they behave in the church.

There are some other things the church should be able to do to help the new pastor get off to a good start: Anytime someone moves into a new setting, there will be unexpected situations that make it difficult to get a job done. In addition to normal hospitality, a church can take some concrete steps to ease the difficulty of adjustment. One thing would be to prepare a directory of community services. This directory should include who's in charge of what service along with phone numbers, email, and other pertinent contact information. This directory might include government officials, child protective services, the Red Cross, police and fire, Salvation Army, hospitals and nursing homes (include chaplains or who to contact about hospital policies on visiting), community food banks and any other community services that the pastor might need to know about.

If the pastor isn't from the general area of the church, it would be helpful to be sure the pastor knows how to contact various denominational officials in the area. Also, it would be helpful to know what ministerial alliances are in the areas (both denominationally oriented and inter-denominationally oriented). On a personal level, it's good to be sure the incoming pastor knows where various stores are and what other services, such as home repair or maintenance, are available. Perhaps it would be helpful to recommend some good mechanics. Don't forget the pastor will most likely need to hook up internet service as well as other utilities.

In general, I avoid recommendations about the settled pastor's first Sunday on the field. At the most, if needed, I suggest the congregation do something to welcome the new pastor into the church and make provisions for people to meet them.

Someone will have to be available to give keys to the pastor. This is one of those things that everyone might assume someone else is doing. Be sure the incoming pastor also knows who to contact regarding music and Sunday bulletins if they are used.

I avoid making recommendations about installation worship services. If nothing is mentioned, I might suggest the church check with the incoming pastor to find out if they want an installation service.

Many of the things above can be handled by the transition team, and it's wise for any Transitional Pastor to avoid dealing with any issues related to the incoming pastor.

Chapter 12:
Cultural Dimensions of Transitional Ministry

TALKING ABOUT "CULTURAL" DIMENSIONS automatically lends itself to misunderstanding. I struggled to find the right word to convey that each congregation develops its own unique characteristics, which in turn affect how the congregation reacts to different situations. These characteristics are understood to be normal by the congregation. However, an interim pastor who comes into a church unaware of these characteristics can end up being at cross purposes with the congregation without really understanding why. In the end, the only word that seemed to fit was "culture."

Intentional Interim and Transitional Ministries, more than any other form of ministry, require a relatively quick assessment of a group's culture in order to make a connection with that group. With a more settled form of ministry, there's time to get to know people, understand the underlying assumptions a particular church culture makes, and test out various approaches. Perhaps more importantly, there's time to let the congregation get to know you in return. Because a transitional pastor is time-limited, there isn't the luxury to take time in building relationships.

A congregation will react to a transitional pastor differently than to a settled pastor. The transitional person is always on the "verge of leaving." I doubt that many congregations, if any, can fully accept a transitional pastor as "pastor." In the back of their mind, and rightly so, there's the idea that this person is temporary. Because of that, they'll limit how much personal energy they put into their relationship with the transitional person.

In part, the job of the interim is to observe a congregation and report back to them on those observations. However, this isn't a "power" role. The congregation is always free to disregard what the transitional pastor reports to them. In that sense, they are in much more of a "consulting" role than a "shepherd" role guiding the flock. To perform this consulting role well requires some understanding of the church's unique culture.

Over the last fifteen years of observing and working with congregations from a transitional ministry position, I have seen three general areas of culture differences. Working with a congregation is easier if you remain aware of these areas where cultural differences in a church may show up.

They are:

1. The congregation's trust in the transitional pastor.
2. How progress is made in a congregation.
3. The beliefs about personal power and hopelessness in a congregation.

Under each of these three headings there are subheadings to expand upon and clarify their meanings.

The Congregation's Trust in the Interim Pastor

Each congregation will have a unique view of the role of the transitional pastor. Those preconceptions will be based on the congregation's past experience. Keep in mind that the transitional pastor will always be an outsider. An "outsider" is someone who isn't a recognized part of the congregation. From the congregation's perspective, the outsider doesn't necessarily have the same values and the outsider may not make the same assumptions as those who are inside the group.

"We must trust the outsider" vs. "We must never trust the outsider"

This aspect of church culture is about how a congregation relates to an outsider. A congregation may find it easier or more difficult to trust an outsider. Be careful here. A transitional pastor may share the same values and assumptions as a particular congregation, but if those perspectives are coming from outside, the congregation won't believe the transitional pastor has them until those values are demonstrated. Being seen as an "outsider" isn't about what the transitional pastor believes, it's about what the members of the congregation believe.

A strongly inwardly-focused congregation may never really trust an outsider. A transitional pastor may fully understand that a church is in pain, and may fully understand that the source of that pain is caused by grief over losing the former pastor, or hurt stemming from actions the former pastor took. However, if the congregation itself doesn't understand the pain they're in, the congregation as a whole may be in a place where they'll never believe the "outsider" understands.

In some cases, it may be that someone from outside the congregation brought pain into the church. That makes it very hard for the congregation to trust anyone coming into the church from the outside.

There are other reasons for distrust of outsiders. One of those reasons may be that the former pastor was personally very insecure. In trying to bolster their own security, there may have been an intentional or covert sewing of distrust of any outsider.

There are clues you can look for to find out if a congregation doesn't trust an outsider. You'll hear things like, "How can they help? They aren't one of us." As far as the individual making the statements is concerned, those questions are valid and not seen as prejudicial toward someone from outside the congregation. The individual who raises the questions might be genuinely surprised their questions are related to trust issues involving an outsider.

Trying to convince the group that the transitional pastor is trustworthy is usually ineffective. Anything that the interim argues will be coming from an outsider and, as such, is suspicious. Building relationships is the best way (perhaps the only way) of overcoming distrust. If the transitional pastor can persevere, being present with people and building connections, then they will come to be seen as part of the group rather than as an outsider.

The "trust versus distrust of an outsider" aspect of church culture has two ends. There can also be an unwarranted *trust* of anyone who isn't part of the congregation. This can happen when there's been so much pain coming from within the congregation that a belief develops that anyone from outside the group will have to be better.

A congregation may be looking for someone to step in and ease or remove their pain. In that case, the outsider is looked to as a savior. This can be a very seductive situation. Every word the transitional pastor says is clung to and every word is seen as a pronouncement from God. If the transitional pastor starts believing their own press, the situation can become very dangerous for both the transitional pastor and the congregation.

From my perspective, God has only appeared in human form once. Even then, some people banded together to kill him. If the transitional pastor starts to believe they have the only answer, it would be wise to keep their eyes open for a cross being erected.

"The outsider is the hero/rescuer" vs. "The outsider is the enemy/destroyer"

The concepts of the "outsider hero" and the "outsider enemy" are closely related to trust versus distrust of the outsider. However, these issues are different enough to warrant examining separately.

Sometimes the outsider is seen as a hero: The transitional pastor is the knight in shining armor sent to rescue the church from whatever has been threatening it. Things in the congregation may be so bad that people begin to believe a rescue *must* come from outside. People in this place have lost faith in their own ability to make change.

At other times, the outsider is the enemy: Because the transitional pastor is an outsider, people may believe the interim is intent on destroying the system. This is most often seen in congregations that are absolutely convinced they're unquestionably right about every stance they have taken. The fear is that their stances may be challenged and, in doing that, they themselves, as individuals, may be devalued.

This category differs from the trust versus distrust of the outsider in that it isn't the ideas or concepts the outsider brings; it's the outsider as an entity separate from the congregation. A congregation may feel little need to listen to what the interim says because their ideas don't matter. It's the very fact that the interim is an outsider that's the determining factor.

The hero vs enemy approach is most likely to occur where there's a belief that the transitional pastor is being forced on the congregation. The force can be direct, as in judicatories where a bishop or other denominational official tells the congregation what's going to happen. It can also be indirect in a situation where a congregation believes a final solution should be made *right now* and the transitional pastor is perceived to be a delaying tactic.

In a purely congregational setting, the hero versus villain reaction is most likely to be seen when the congregation is polarized. In that case, one faction within a congregation may see another faction as having imposed their desires on the congregation as a whole. In this case, the interim faces a difficult task in reconciling the two groups before a new settled pastor is on the scene.

When you look for this mindset in a congregation, watch for groups of individuals who hang out together and who do not welcome those outside their own group. That's especially true if the interim isn't invited to join one group and is made to feel special in another group.

"The outsider is being honest and transparent" vs. "The outsider is being manipulative and self-serving"

The third aspect, which is closely related to trust issues, has to do with the motivation of the outsider. If a congregation has a strongly suspicious nature, the outsider may be assumed to be manipulative and self-serving. This can be very hard to overcome because the assumption is that anything the transitional pastor says has an ulterior motive.

In these cases, facts are of little value. The assumption will be that "facts" are selected to support an ulterior motive or that the facts aren't actually facts. We've seen this phenomenon when people hear news they don't like and they automatically classify it as fake news. The same is true in this case.

It's also possible for a group to have the opposite tendency to believe that the outsider is always being honest and transparent. This assumption is usually seen in groups that have had high internal conflict that was unresolved. They simply don't believe they can trust each other and therefore, if anyone can be trusted, it has to be someone from outside the system.

"You have to speak in our common language" vs. "You have to not speak in our common language"

The term "language" here goes deeper than a specific spoken language such as English or Spanish. Within each language group, there are variations in which words are used most frequently as well as the connotations of those words. A group may put together a particular set of words, idioms, and connotative meanings to form a language of their own. This set of words and use of words might be considered a vernacular. When a vernacular is in place over a long period of time, there ceases to be an awareness of the words or concepts as anything other than totally normal and right. Other words and idioms are likely to be considered wrong.

One example might be the use of the word "narthex." It's a common word describing a particular part of a church building, usually the area that leads into the sanctuary. Even if this definition is acceptable to a group, the use of the term "narthex" can be problematic.

A traditional congregational protestant may see "narthex" as a word associated with high church traditions. Others may see it as simply being descriptive. Even the phrase "high church" has a variety of meanings. In some congregations, the term will be similar to "ritualistic" or "liberal." Other churches see it as reflective of a style of worship, not directly related to a theological stance or the enthusiasm of worship.

All of these connotative meanings—words that are commonly used and the idioms that are a part of the communication patterns of a congregation—go into making up that congregation's unique vernacular. These words will produce emotional responses that are understood as the "right" thing to do or say. If this were applied to a geographical region, one might call it a dialect. However, the way I'm using it here is more specified because it's applied to individual congregations. Calling it a dialect might lead one to think it can be easily interpreted and understood outside of the congregation.

The congregational language that's prevalent can either facilitate the work of the transitional pastor or derail it completely. In some groups, the congregational language becomes so central to the congregation's identity that any variation in language is considered a threat to the group's existence. A group might believe that any language other than what they're comfortable with indicates a basic disagreement with their core principles.

Early in my ministry I encountered an individual who was set on a particular way words were used. He asked to record a few sermons and then took the recordings to the board of deacons as proof I wasn't preaching the gospel. He pointed out that I never used the term "Lord Jesus Christ." Because I didn't use that exact term, I didn't believe in Jesus as Lord of the church.

Among the sermons he had recorded was one I preached from Philippians 2:5-11. The entire focus of the message was on the last verse saying everyone will proclaim Jesus Christ is Lord. Luckily for me, there were men on the board of deacons who were wise enough to point out that the ideas were the same and there could be no question where I stood. The complaining individual didn't see it that way. To him, "Lord Jesus Christ" and "Jesus Christ is Lord" were totally different in meaning.

If a transitional pastor uses different language, the congregation may well look at the transitional pastor as being an outsider and a danger. They listen to the transitional pastor's language and because they don't hear their own vocabulary and idioms, they may discount what's being said.

This can be particularly tricky. Sometimes we make decisions about who someone is based on nothing more than who they appear to be identified with. The term "Baptist" carries a lot of connotations. I sometimes have to explain that I'm an "American Baptist" because people hear "Baptist" and assume I'm like the Baptists who demonstrate at funerals or that I share all the views of Southern Baptists. The Southern Baptist connection is complicated by the fact that I graduated from Southern Baptist Theological Seminary in Louisville, Kentucky.

Related to these identifying terms is the concept of "reputation." A congregation may have a reputation that disposes a transitional pastor to pre-judge what the church will be like and what the congregation will listen to. The other side of the coin is that the congregation may also have pre-judgments about an interim minster. Once those pre-judgments are active, the language used by either party will be looked at from the standpoint of those pre-judgments.

There's also the possibility in a congregation of the opposite problem. In my experience, it's much less common. The congregation may realize they have reached a place where their understanding of a situation isn't sufficient. In that case, using different vocabulary and idioms may be what the group is actually looking for. Using the same congregational language may lead to the congregation assuming the transitional pastor is simply repeating the same old story and as a result they may dismiss what the transitional pastor has to say. Saying things in a modified congregational language may give the congregation hope something can be different.

The transitional pastor needs to have an idea of the congregational language and how it differs with the transitional pastor's way of communication. In some ways, this needs to be done by instinct. By that I mean the transitional pastor will need to have enough experience that conversational reactions (a frown, a grimace, a smile, a nod of the head), or verbal responses will give clues to how the hearer is understanding what's being said.

In order to communicate, it will be necessary to understand the vernacular of a congregation and to adjust to that vernacular. If the transitional pastor's vernacular isn't recognized, people in the congregation may make up their own minds about what the transitional pastor is saying and reject it out of hand or resist anything the transitional pastor is trying to do. Once that happens, it's very hard for them to reconsider what they've already decided.

"The stated reasons are the final truth" vs. "The stated reasons are always hiding something"

If you pay attention to the news media, you'll be very well aware of how the word "truth" can be manipulated. There's a tendency on the part of some to listen to a story and proclaim what they hear as "true." Others listen to the same story and proclaim that it isn't the whole story. They'll spend a lot effort trying to find the real reason (the "actual truth") behind what was reported. People justify this perspective by saying whatever truth was presented was intended to be misleading.

This cultural aspect within a church is hard to define. All sides are almost always stating the truth as they perceive it to be. For example, a former pastor may have focused on preaching and minimized the amount of in-home visiting they did. The congregation may complain that the pastor didn't care about the people in the church because there wasn't "enough" time spent on visiting congregation members. But a different congregation may have the same pastor and see the effort put into preparing sermons as an indication the pastor cared very deeply about the congregation's well-being.

For the transitional pastor, the task is to sort through the reasoning behind the "truth" that each side presents and see if there are similar issues underlying each proclamation of the "truth." (Note that the task isn't about finding the "real truth." Finding the "real truth" is a trail that leads nowhere.)

A congregation may also jump to conclusions based on perceived "truths." When different groups within a congregation have different perceptions of "the truth"—and what decisions should be made based upon those "truths"—the result can be conflict and separation. Once a group within a congregation has determined what the truth is, that group will want decisions made based upon their own perspective. That's all well and good as long as the groups involved don't decide that their way is the *only* way. The reality is that there are always subtleties to every problem and those subtleties need to be kept in mind.

The opposite end of this issue involves the belief that there's always some hidden factor that hasn't been examined. If those other factors, "the other truths," aren't taken into account, the church may end up repeating previous mistakes. If the church focuses on finding "the other truths," and assumes "the other truths" are essential to find before moving on, the church can become paralyzed, going over reasons again and again, trying to be sure they're acting on the *ultimate* truth.

The transitional pastor has a difficult job in these situations. The interim may find issues that need to be challenged that aren't within the scope of issues the congregation considers important.

In order to make progress, the congregation may *need* to examine additional truths to get to the heart of the matter. At the same time, the transitional pastor will need to tread carefully. If the focus strays too far into finding "other truths," there's a risk of the church becoming paralyzed by their search and not taking positive action.

How Progress Is Made in a Congregation

Progress is movement toward a desired goal. This does not necessarily refer to change. The goal of a congregation can be to remain the same. Progress is then defined in terms of what suppresses change. There are a variety of things that can affect how progress is made. Core beliefs are one of the things that can hinder or help progress.

A "core belief" is a belief that is basic to a group. A core belief isn't debatable from the group's point of view. It isn't debatable because, for the group, it's a self-evident truth. No one can disagree with a core belief, at least no one the group wants to have as a leader. A core belief may not even be in the conscious awareness of the group, but the belief will affect how a group moves forward or remains the same.

A transitional pastor will encounter core beliefs that effect how the congregation reacts to them. It's unlikely that these core beliefs will be changed in a short period between pastors. However, being aware of some of these beliefs may allow the transitional pastor to choose a strategy that will allow progress despite the core belief. Choosing the wrong strategy will result in gridlock.

Below are several possible core beliefs that a transitional pastor will have to work with in order to accomplish their purpose. This list is not exhaustive. There may well be other beliefs an interim may encounter based on their location and the unique congregation.

This is not a cook book approach that will tell you, "Do this when confronting this particular core belief." My intention is for the reader to become aware of different core beliefs that are on the opposite ends of a spectrum. The transitional pastor will have to call on their own professional expertise to decide how to deal with a situation.

"The organization/institution is primary" vs. "The individual is primary"

When working with a church in transition, two important questions are: "How important is the church as an institution?" and "How important are the individual persons within the church?" Another way to ask that is: "Which is more important: the wellbeing of the institution or the wellbeing of individuals within the institution?" There's an old saying that, "Some people eat to live, others live to eat." This could be paraphrased to mean that some churches serve people so the church can exist and some churches exist so people can be served.

Understanding which is primary is important when working with a church. If they perceive the transitional pastor to be interested in relationships with people when their interest is in the institution, it's unlikely the church will hear what the transitional pastor has to say. Obviously, the reverse is also true.

It's normal to think of an institution as being composed of the people who make it up. Individuals make up the legal or formal organization. However, there's another object that can also represent the institution of the church. It isn't unusual for the church building itself to represent the people in the congregation. That can result in the congregation defining itself by the way the building looks. The better the building looks, the better people in the congregation feel about themselves. At times, the main reason (usually unconscious and rarely, if ever, stated) for getting new people to be a part of the congregation is so the building can be maintained.

This attitude can be antithetical to the stated mission of a church: to bring people into the kingdom of God. The congregation may vehemently deny that they have placed the building as their first priority. Yet, if it comes to a choice about preserving the building as opposed to bringing in new people, if preserving the building wins, then it's probable the real focus of the church is serving the institution first.

I've heard stories of ministries formed to bring people into the church that are scrapped when there's damage to the church building. One example would be a youth ministry that's going well, bringing unchurched youth to the church. Then a window gets broken, or someone writes on a bathroom wall, or someone damages a member's car in the parking lot and the ministry is shut down. The defense offered is that the congregation needs to be a good steward of what they have.

The same comparison can be made between the mission of the church and the church building. Some churches are committed to keeping the mission of the church the same as it's always been. That's commendable if the mission is still serving a verifiable need. But sometimes a mission has been accomplished and it's no longer needed. That may be because the demographics change so that the mission, while still valid for some settings, is no longer needed where the church is located. There may be a need to focus on a different mission or group of people. If the "mission" is primary, it will be hard for people to hear that it has to change.

Another way of looking at this is whether the individual needs or the institutional needs are of primary importance. Imagine a church that has multiple levels (floors) and requires stairs to move between levels. An elevator can only be installed in one location and the installation of the elevator in that location would negatively impact the way the church looks both inside and out. If the church continues expecting people to use stairs because of the aesthetic ramifications of installing an elevator, then the needs of the church building are more important than the needs of the individuals who attend that church (or of visitors who may be interested in attending).

Unfortunately, this dimension is rarely, if ever, as clear cut as what I've laid out above. The transitional pastor has to watch for subtle clues that may be interpreted in differing ways. If a church has a community kitchen ministry where people are fed and the objection is made, "None of those people ever come to the church," then it's possible the church as an institution is more important than the people being served.

"Carefully thought out and planned strategies" vs. "Do something right now strategies"

Different churches approach things differently. Some churches approach things in a systematic, carefully thought out way. They take care to let everyone know what steps are being taken to accomplish a goal. This may be accompanied by flow charts, written plans, and regular progress reports.

Other churches will find this approach to be smothering. In these churches, what's important is that something obvious is being accomplished. If there are several things started that have to be abandoned, that's okay as long as progress is being made. While most churches claim to want the carefully thought out approach, they may in actuality favor the "just do something" approach.

An initial presentation to a church from an Intentional Interim perspective will most likely include a carefully laid out plan of action. However, if the church is used to a "just doing something" approach, after a time there will be resistance to the carefully planned out approach.

The difference between carefully-thought-out-action and just-doing-something is a major difficulty for a pastoral search committee. To do a proper search requires effort. Unfortunately, there are times when a church appoints a committee to do the pastoral search, then when the committee follows a carefully laid out course of action, the church gets upset that the process is taking too long.

Either approach (just do something or plan carefully) can work. And either approach can have negative effects on the health of a congregation. If the "just do something" approach is carried to an extreme, the results can be a lot of action with little substantive results. There'll be a trail of false starts that consume resources and drain the energies of the people doing the work.

The systematic approach can also be detrimental if all the effort is spent on laying out the system. At some point, action has to be taken or nothing will get done. Understanding how the church functions in this way will help the transitional pastor understand how to approach changes that need to be made.

"Don't think about alternatives" vs. "Don't stop thinking about alternatives"

This may be a corollary to the "carefully thought out and planned strategies" versus the "do something right now strategies." As soon as a possible course of action is proposed and met with some approval, a congregation can put on blinders to keep them from seeing any other possibility for action. Any alternative is seen as a distraction.

A church may have resources that will help them make decisions. However, if they're in the "don't think about alternatives" camp, the church may never even consider that they have alternatives that have worked for them or other congregations in the past. It isn't unusual for a congregation to act as if they've already considered all the relevant alternatives about how to approach an issue and not want to look at anything new.

If a church has adopted the "we already know the right answers" approach, the interim minster's job is to help them understand there may be other possible ways to approach a problem. The transitional pastor needs to be careful not to convey the idea that the transitional pastor has the one true answer to their problem.

The other side of the coin appears when the church is so concerned over finding the "correct answer" that they can't stop thinking of alternatives. If that happens, there's a danger they will never get anything done. Every idea is examined over and over, searching for the "one" right answer. The transitional pastor's job is to push the church to make a decision without dictating what that decision should be.

Part of the education the church needs from the Intentional Interim or Transitional Pastor is that a wrong decision isn't catastrophic.

"Gut instinct is most highly valued" vs. "Scientific information is most highly valued"

When trying to decide what may be beneficial to a congregation or, conversely, may be harmful to a congregation, there are two ways the decision can be approached. One way is to look at the hard facts. The other way is to trust "gut instinct."

The "scientific" approach means the congregation looks at evidence, numbers, and research articles to show them what will be the "right" answer. In some congregations that may be the primary way of going about the decision-making process. If a new copier is being considered, for example, there will be a search for recommendations and price lists from various places.

However, in recent years our society has undergone a major shift in thinking. "Facts" are not seen as objective truths, but rather, the "facts" have become "what feels good to me." This is actually an opinion approach and has nothing to do with science.

The problem with the opinion approach is that if someone believes one thing and someone else sees things differently, objective facts are of little value. "Facts" that "feel bad" can be dismissed so that the "facts" that feel good can be sustained. The gut instinct approach may work if the congregation is relatively homogeneous. In that case, they'll probably share some gut instincts and there won't be any problem. The approach only becomes a problem if the gut instinct approach leads a congregation in a direction that will be harmful. The "scientific" approach may offer some help, but it will likely be rejected out of hand.

For the interim pastor, this can be a minefield. People won't be persuaded by the "truth." To attempt to persuade one side of an issue using the tools of the other side won't work. To say, "Here's what research shows," to a group that bases its decisions on gut instinct is almost guaranteed to fail. Just the phrasing can set up automatic defenses. The opposite is also true: If an organization is research-and-statistics oriented in their decision-making process, to talk about what you "feel" will be an invitation to dismiss what you have to say.

The reality is that if you want to be effective, you also have to decide what issues are worth a struggle and what issues will never change.

"Past is prologue" vs. "Past is determinative"

One of the Focus Points I bring to a congregation involves the church's heritage. Most congregations believe they have a good grasp on their heritage. However, even if a good look at the heritage of the church was done before the last pastor came, and even if that pastor was there for only a few months, the heritage of the church has been altered. A congregation does well to consider how recent experiences have altered the understanding of the church's heritage. I'm not saying the foundational heritage will change, but the understanding and effect of it will change.

Some churches understand heritage as being a guidepost to the future. They understand their particular heritage as actually leading them forward into the future. That is undoubtedly true. Our heritage will always set the direction for the future. That future may include dealing with portions of the church's heritage that hinder the church from moving forward. When a church has an orientation that says the past is prologue, then a careful understanding of the past is critical. The heritage of the past will be helpful only to the extent that it's understood.

Some churches will be on the other end of the spectrum that says the past is an absolute, it cannot change and it determines what the church will do in the future. No matter what anyone does, what has happened before is what will happen again. This is another aspect—similar to "hopefulness versus despair," which I will discuss later in the text—that can be hidden under a dogma that proclaims, "God can change anything," while the actual underlying belief may be that events have been set in motion that will play out to an inevitable end. Change isn't possible.

The transitional pastor is in the place of advocating for both of these positions. There's no doubt the particular heritage of a congregation will have an impact on future decisions. It isn't unusual for a congregation to be unaware of how their heritage is impacting them. The transitional pastor can facilitate the congregation in becoming aware of how their heritage is affecting the future and that the future doesn't have to be written by the past.

The Beliefs About Personal Power and Hopelessness in a Congregation

The *perceived* power of individuals and of the congregation is an important aspect of the church's culture. This has been true from the very beginning of the church. Jesus had to deal with personal power issues among the disciples. It came out as James and John wanting special, privileged positions.[7]

Understanding the power dynamics in a church will contribute to a successful transitional ministry.

"Personal powerlessness" vs. "Personal power"

Individuals within a congregation will have beliefs about their ability to affect outcomes in the church. This is a "personal power" dimension. The belief about the effectiveness of personal power is a result of events that have transpired in an individual's life. On the organizational level, the perceived level of personal power is the result of significant events in the church's past. I cannot imagine any organization or church ever being formed if its members believed they couldn't really change anything. However, once formed, the church may decide they actually have much less ability to bring about change than they originally thought.

The "personal" part of "personal powerlessness" or "personal power" may refer to a whole congregation that is somehow a subset of a larger organization (i.e., a congregation that is part of a denomination). However, it can also refer to one individual or a small group of individuals within the church (i.e., a Sunday school class or a particular team or board within the church). I will be

---

7   Mark 10:35-45

referring to "congregations" or "churches" in what follows, but keep in mind it could be translated as individuals too.

If, over time, a congregation tries to make changes in their community and time after time those changes fail to take hold, personal powerlessness can become the dominate characteristic of the church. Any suggested change in the church may be met with skepticism or even hostility. The hostility may come from attempting to avoid failure one more time.

Personal powerlessness can be expressed as hostility, but may also manifest as people simply being worn out—no one seems to have the energy to try again. An excuse sometimes offered is that circumstances have changed and individuals within the congregation can no longer do what's needed.

Even basic evangelism can become the precipitating cause of this attitude shift. People may have been brought to the church and the membership may have grown. Then, for any number of reasons, the membership may drop. It may be that the congregation ages and those who were active before are no longer able to be active and there isn't a new generation of people to step up to the plate. The drop in congregational membership could be because there were major social changes—perhaps a major manufacturing plant moved out of town and many of the church members moved with it, for example. The reason for the change isn't as important as recognizing that the change exists.

It depends on the unique issues of a church whether personal power is a positive or negative influence. It can always be hoped that a congregation will have a sense that they can accomplish things, that they are powerful and able to affect the future.

If the congregation is operating from a position of personal powerlessness, then the transitional pastor will have to reinforce their sense of personal power as a congregation. At the same time, the transitional pastor will have to monitor the situation to see that the congregation and/or individuals within the congregation aren't coming to believe they are omnipotent.

"Hopefulness" vs. "Despair"

This dimension is related to the "personal power" versus "personal powerlessness" dimension, but focuses more on personal responsibility. The driving belief in "personal power" is that the individual has the power to bring about change. The driving force in the personal powerlessness end of the continuum is that the individual can't effect change at all. When these beliefs are carried to the extreme, then there may be despair because nothing can bring about any change, *or* blind hopefulness will prevail despite serious setbacks.

Either extreme can be a problem for a church in transition. Some churches seem to adopt a defeatist attitude that says the church is dead. The majority feel there's nothing that can be done so it's best to accept "reality" and wait for the burial. I see this in a lot of small churches that have been experiencing decline for several years. Even in calling a new settled pastor, they don't really believe anything positive is going to happen. In effect, the church is going through the motions without really anticipating anything will change.

Extreme hopefulness can also be a problem. That may sound strange, but if a church adopts a Pollyanna-ish attitude that says everything will be okay, even if they don't do anything, then a disaster could be in the making. The church may not take any responsibility for what may change; it's all left to "the powers that be."

It's unusual for an Intentional Interim Pastor or Transitional Pastor to be called in when despair has totally overtaken a church. In order for a transitional pastor to be effective, there must be at least *some* hopefulness. It may be a very small amount of hope, but any hope at all will give you a place to start.

These extremes are often disguised when making first contact with a church. Dogma might say there's always hope and people should rely on God to fix things. To admit despair is to admit to having lost one's faith. The congregation may present as very hopeful, but when carefully examined, hopefulness is found to be a cover for despair. If it turns out the church truly is in total despair, the interim's job may be to help them have a good closure.

The transitional pastor has to negotiate the waters between the two extremes, much like the waters between personal power and personal powerlessness. There's a need to let the congregation become aware of how they're approaching things, but that's easier said than done. The words "let the congregation become aware" are used very intentionally. It's usually counterproductive to try and "tell" the congregation or directly educate the congregation about their hopefulness or despair.

If the congregation is completely embedded in absolute hopefulness, I find it best to help them discover what concrete actions they've taken in the past to accomplish a goal. I help them to see, again usually indirectly, that they need to put a lot of effort into the whole transition process.

Similarly, if the congregation is in extreme despair, I want them to see what has happened in the past. I want them to examine situations that looked absolutely hopeless and see what members of the congregation did in those times to move beyond their despair.

"Guilt" vs. "Not responsible"

The final aspect I want to touch on is the idea of "guilt" versus "not responsible." There may be any number of things that happen to a congregation which result in either of these two reactions. Regardless, they need to be taken into consideration.

Churches as well as individuals may be overwhelmed by guilt. A pastor may suddenly die or become ill, there may be a major boundary violation in the church not involving a pastor, there may be a conflict that has been going on for many years. Undoubtedly there will be individual reactions, but there can also be congregation-wide reactions. As with every dimension of church culture, there will undoubtedly be people on both sides of the continuum. The transitional pastor needs to be aware of where the majority of the energy in the church is located.

What makes this dimension so tricky to deal with is that, regardless of the cause, both ends of the continuum are most likely valid at some level. For instance, say a pastor suddenly dies of a heart attack. The church may have encouraged or ignored a stressful circumstance in the church which was a contributing factor to the pastor's heart attack. Sometimes the stress can be very direct and observable by everyone. At other times, the stress might not be recognized until after the fact. Perhaps the church's contribution to that stress is never seen.

The church may descend into a crippling guilt where everyone, or an important segment of the congregation, will engage in breast-beating—not only acknowledging their part in producing the situation, but seeing their part as being totally responsible for what happened.

The opposite extreme would involve the pastor being given total responsibility for the stressful circumstance. There might be blaming statements such as, "He didn't take care of himself physically," or "She took everything too seriously." The church won't take any responsibility for producing or perpetuating the stress that contributed to the heart attack.

The reality is that, in most situations, both things are true. A church can set up a scenario which contributes to a pastor having a heart attack, *and* the pastor sets the stage regardless of what the church does. The same can be said for situations where a pastor is involved in boundary violations or has their own family crisis (e.g., divorce).

The transitional pastor will need to help the church or the differing groups within a church to accept their responsibility and to let go of what isn't their responsibility. The difficulty is in bringing people into balance and not moving a group from one pole to the polar opposite.

A congregation can be responsible for having taken some action that resulted in the pastor leaving. That action may or may not have been with the intention of forcing the pastor to leave. The reason for the action is secondary. What's important is that the congregation as a whole will need to deal with forgiveness or a lack of forgiveness. In this case, it's self-forgiveness.

When the church in some way precipitated the leaving of a pastor, there's a whole new dimension that will be beneficial for the transitional pastor to know about: "forgive" versus "unforgivable." This is true even when the reason for the pastor leaving required action on the part of the church to terminate the relationship.

If a pastor was involved in a boundary violation of a sexual nature, there's no choice but for the church to end the relationship. While it's possible that the church set up an environment that was conducive to the actions of the pastor, the actions themselves are the pastor's responsibility and there should be no attempt to excuse those actions. Despite this, a church may still feel a sense of guilt.

I used the above example because it's one where many would say there's absolutely no need for the congregation to feel guilt. The point is that a congregation may feel guilt even if there's no need. The transitional pastor will need to be aware of that possibility.

In the case of ongoing guilt, rational or not, it's important for people to once again understand the concept of grace as applied to themselves. It's often easier to be gracious and forgiving of someone else than of ourselves.

Chapter 13:
Conflict as a Part of Transitional Ministries

CONFLICT IS A NATURAL PART OF LIFE and we can find it just about everywhere we go. There's conflict in the animal kingdom, the working of natural forces, and in the clash of spiritual forces. Even though many people see conflict as being "unspiritual," even congregations have conflict. An interim pastor will most likely have to deal with some level of conflict.

If I were to boil all the origins of conflict down into a single word, that word would be "fear." In the end, all human conflict is the result of fear on the part of the parties involved. The fear may be of losing power or of someone else gaining power (which may result in the one who is fearful losing power). It may be a fear of losing influence (which is also a form of power).

Conflict may also come because of a change in the way things are done. Change always produces fear at some level. The transition from one settled pastor to another is a major change in any congregation's life. It can be assumed there will be fear, and potentially conflict, when a congregation is transitioning between pastors.

There are four basic aspects of conflict to keep in mind. First, you have to be aware of the groupings of the conflict. Secondly, you have to be aware of the issues of the conflict. Third, you have to be aware of the contextual features of the conflict. Finally, you have to be aware of the escalating nature of the conflict. Keeping these four aspects in mind will help you in dealing with conflict in a congregation.

Also keep in mind, when dealing with any conflict, the *apparent* cause of the conflict may or may not be the *actual* cause of the conflict. It isn't unusual to find out the issue that's brought up as the source of disagreement is really a way of justifying a conflict about some other issue. Johnny and Joey may be in conflict over something like putting a basketball hoop in the parking lot. The actual source of the conflict may go all the way back to Johnny's father and Joey's father both trying to date the same girl in high school, and their sons carried on the rivalry. The actual source of a conflict may never be discovered, but what you can do is help people think through the apparent conflict so life can go on.

I don't usually refer to conflict resolution. Rather, I prefer to call it conflict transformation. When I first started using that term twenty years ago, I thought it was original to me. I later found out it was a term used by several people. The idea behind using the word "transformation" instead of "resolution" is that conflict isn't always bad. At times, conflict drives things forward. "Resolution" of conflict means the conflict ceases to exist. It's more helpful if the conflict can "transform" into something that moves the parties or the institution involved forward.

I once prepared a workbook for a "Conflict Transformation Workshop." On the front was a picture with raging whitewater foam amidst otherwise quiet water. The picture was taken from the back of a cruise ship. The whitewater is produced by the propeller driving the ship forward.

The Groupings of Conflict

One way to differentiate types of conflict is on the basis of who's involved in the conflict. A conflict can be an individual conflict, a group conflict, or a mixture of the two.

Individual conflicts exist where two or more individuals are in conflict. Group conflicts involve two or more groups of people in conflict. The more complex the groupings, the more difficult it will be to deal with a conflict.

An individual conflict is fairly easy to conceptualize: two or more individuals are in conflict with each other. There will be something that the individuals involved want that apparently can't be obtained if the other individual gets what they want.

Group conflicts involve two or more groups with each group made up of two or more individuals. Group conflicts have the same dynamic as individual conflicts: fear that if Group Alpha gets what it wants, Broup Beta will be denied what it wants. The major difference is that there's now a *group* of people who are defining what is wanted.

A group develops a life of its own. A group will have characteristics very similar to an individual involved in an individual conflict. However, despite apparent agreement within a group about they want, there may not be a real consensus. It may be that some elements of the group align themselves with a sub-group hoping to get the larger group to support their agenda. Any agreement reached within a larger group can fall apart when those sub-groups start demanding what they want.

Whether you're dealing with an individual or group conflict, in order for transformation to take place, it's necessary to grasp the apparent reason for the conflict and, if possible, the underlying reasons behind the conflict. It may not be necessary to have everyone agree or even be able to articulate the underlying cause; but there's a risk, if the underlying cause isn't known, that the conflict may appear to be finished only to reappear in some other arena.

A basic fact of life is that each individual, whether acting as an individual or as a part of a group, carries a personal history. That history may include things the individual would rather not admit to being a part of their life. Carl Jung referred to underlying forces in someone's personal history as "shadow." These unseen forces will color how individuals see a situation and will often be the real reason for a conflict. In many cases, an individual will be unaware of that history and/or shadow.

A group of people will come together because of common interests. It's also true that common shadows can be another element bonding a group together. In some cases, the shadow will be a stronger influence than any openly-expressed concern simply because the shadow isn't obvious and thus works at an unconscious level.

Contrary to what you might intuit, it's often harder to get at those shadows in an individual conflict than in a group conflict. In an individual conflict, the individuals bring only their own perspective, governed by their own personal history, to the table. There's only one person who can give evidence as to what the shadow might be. In a group conflict, each member of the group brings their unique perspective to the table. Because the perspectives within a group are different, it may be easier to spot common themes which may relate to the ongoing conflict.

Even if it's easier to spot "shadow" in a group conflict, it isn't easier to deal with. In an individual conflict, you only have to deal with the shadow of the individual. In the group conflict, you have to deal with all the individual shadows in the group as well as the group shadow inherent in that particular group.

It's also possible to have a combination of an individual and group conflict. In this case, an individual is in conflict with a group. Here a facilitator will have to be aware of and work with all of the advantages and disadvantages associated with both an individual conflict and a group conflict.

To further complicate matters, either a group or individual conflict may disguise itself as the other. It may appear that two individuals have squared off against each other for some reason, let's say it's about the proverbial color of the church carpet. The conflict may appear to be strictly between these two individuals. However, when examined more closely, you may find out that each individual has a constituency within the church that's the actual driving force behind the conflict. In this case, what appears to be an individual conflict is actually a group conflict.

It's also possible that what appears to be group conflict is actually an individual conflict. This happens when an individual enlists the support of other people for their cause. The people so enlisted may not have a lot of investment in what's going on. They're acting out of loyalty to one or the other individual.

Issues of Conflict

A conflict can also be characterized in terms of the basic issues involved. Five of these issues are identified here: *issues of belief, issues of control, issues of rights, issues of identity,* and *issues of faith.* It's necessary to identify which basic issues are involved and address those issues. Once again, keep in mind the apparent issue may not be the actual driving issue in a given conflict. It's important that the interim keep reviewing which issue is driving the conflict.

1) Issues of Belief

Issues of belief are in some ways the easiest to deal with. You need to keep in mind a clear distinction between "belief" and "faith." The term "belief" as used here is about what a person intellectually believes to be true. An *issue of belief* arises when one party (an individual or group) believes one thing to be factually verifiable and another party believes that same thing to *not* be factually verifiable. A facilitator need only find a way to establish what's verifiable and the conflict will be ended. The key issue is to find a means of confirming factual validity that will satisfy both parties. True conflicts of belief are rare. Often what appears to be an *issue of belief* is merely window dressing for one of the other issues of conflict. In order for it to be a true *issue of belief* conflict, there must be a verifiable fact at the center of the conflict.

In recent years, there has been an increase in what appears to be *issues of belief.* An individual or group of individuals will hold onto one belief and another individual or group of individuals will hold onto another belief. Any information that may seem to factually put one belief or the other in jeopardy will be denied. When an individual or a group refuses to accept something as verification of the other party's belief, the conflict has moved to a different stage. In these cases, trying to find out which belief is correct is a futile effort.

2) Issues of Control

In my experience, more often than not, what appears to be an *issue of belief* is actually an *issue of control*. Control conflicts, sometimes referred to as power conflicts, come out of the need for individuals to control their life and their space. The fear here is usually related to survival in one form or another. It's a fear that if a person doesn't have control of a situation (if they don't have enough power), then someone else will use power against them.

The difficulty in dealing with control conflicts is that people don't recognize fear as driving the conflict. Often individuals will think they're dealing with a belief conflict. There's the mistaken assumption that once the belief is established, then the conflict will end. The risk in attempting to intervene in this type of conflict is that the parties involved may view any action taken as an attack on their power and ultimately on their survival.

3) Issues of Rights

Closely related to *issues of control* are *issues of rights*. In *issues of rights* conflicts, there will be an assertion by one individual or group that some inalienable right has been infringed upon by another individual or group. The fear here seems to be that a person will miss out on something they have a right to. In the long run, this is related to the survival of that person's identity.

4) Issues of Identity

The fourth issue of conflict identified here concerns *issues of identity*. How we see and understand ourselves to be in the world is vital. A person will die for their sense of identity. In *issues of identity* there will be something that threatens the world view of an individual or group of individuals in such a way that they're at risk of losing their identity as individuals or as a group. In order for conflict transformation to happen, the individuals or groups involved will have to define their identity in such a way that they protect themselves without threatening the other party(ies) in the conflict.

5) Issues of Faith

The most difficult type of conflict to deal with involves *issues of faith*. In *issues of faith*, there's no absolute, scientific, or physical evidence to which a person can appeal. What's being dealt with are issues of a spiritual nature. Note that in this context, "spiritual" doesn't necessarily mean "religious." The fear that drives faith conflicts can be even more powerful than the fear of survival. The fear of survival is centered on the here and now. In faith conflicts, the focus of the fear has to do with eternity. If a conflict is regarding faith, the person who's trying to facilitate a transformation of that conflict is literally trying to move heaven and hell.

It should be noted the division of the issues of conflict into the five categories identified above is mainly for convenience. In most church conflicts, there's a mixing of the issues. The transitional pastor will have to be aware of the focal issue or issues at each stage of dealing with the conflict.

Context of Conflict

Every conflict has factors which will impede or support the transformation of that conflict into something useful. These factors form the context associated with a particular conflict. There are six factors that determine the context of a conflict.

Factor One: Level of Independence

The first factor is the level of interdependence of the parties involved in the conflict. This is the extent the parties involved in the conflict are interdependent on one another or independent of one another. If the parties need each other to accomplish some task, there's a high degree of interdependence. There are times when the parties in a conflict really need each other. It may be because of a financial situation, a skills situation, or something else where a mutual need for each other exists between the parties.

There are other times when the parties to a conflict are thrown together by circumstances. If not for the accident of their circumstances, each party would be able to function without regard to the other party(ies). However, circumstances force the parties to deal with each other and they each see the other as being a hindrance to accomplishing their goals. In this case, there's a high level of independence.

When there's a high level of interdependence in a conflict, each party will have some understanding of what they need from each other. When both parties need something of nearly equal value from each other to accomplish their goals, the task may be easier. All that may be needed is for the parties to acknowledge their mutual needs.

If the parties are truly independent of each other in terms of what they each need, the conflict can be very difficult to resolve. In this case, there will be a very low level of motivation on the part of parties to see each other's needs and to transform the conflict into something beneficial.

Factor Two: The Number of Parties Involved

A second factor that sets the context of a conflict is whether there are multiple parties involved. "Multiple parties" refers to three or more separate parties involved in the conflict. The conflict could be between three or more individuals, three or more groups, or some combination of three or more groups and individuals. The more parties there are to the conflict, the more difficult it becomes to bring about transformation. This difficulty comes from multiple interactions between each of the parties. In a two-part conflict, there's only one interaction: A↔B. If there are three parties involved, there now are three relationships to consider: A↔B, A↔C, C↔B. In a three-party situation, parties A and B may figure out how to transform the conflict into something beneficial, and parties B and C may make a similar breakthrough, yet parties A and C may still be at odds. If there are four parties involved, it gets even more complicated. There's now: A↔B, A↔C, A↔D, B↔C, B↔D, C↔D.

I was once involved in a conflict in a church setting that exemplified the multi-party conflict situation. The conflict primarily involved leadership personalities. When visitors came to the church, they were asked if they were on the side of Mr. Smith or on the side of Mr. Jones. Both Mr. Smith and Mr. Jones were powerful, successful businessmen. They weren't in direct competition in business, but they were in competition for leadership in the church. At first glance, this appeared to be a two-party conflict, but a third party was involved. This party didn't have a specific leader around which it was focused.

The third party had its own agenda for the church and would work for or against either Mr. Smith or Mr. Jones depending on the third party's agenda. In order to transform the conflict into something beneficial, it was necessary to work with all three parties.

Factor Three: Level of Urgency

A third factor in understanding the context of conflict is the urgency of the issues involved. When the issues of the conflict are urgent in nature, a very different situation exists than if the issues aren't particularly urgent. There are two elements in determining the urgency of an issue: irrevocability and immediacy. An issue is urgent only if there will be an irrevocable consequence, such as one party winning out over the other party. If there isn't such a consequence, the issue isn't urgent. Secondly, for an issue to be considered urgent, there must be a time constraint (immediacy), requiring action on the issue within the very near future. If there's no time constraint, the issue isn't urgent.

As long as the situation isn't urgent, there's plenty of time to let the conflict work itself out. For example, consider an abandoned barn that's of no value. The barn might be taking up space that could be used otherwise, but there's nothing of value inside the barn. If the barn catches fire and there's no danger of the fire spreading to anything else, the situation wouldn't be urgent. However, imagine the same old barn with a new barn full of equipment right next to it. Then the situation becomes urgent. If something isn't done quickly (immediacy) about the old barn that's on fire, the fire will spread to the new barn resulting in the loss of the new barn and the equipment (irrevocability).

Factor Four: Communication Structures

Another factor making up the context of a particular conflict is the communication structure between the parties involved in the conflict. Dialogue is an essential part of conflict transformation. If there's a possibility for face-to-face, immediate communication between the parties in conflict, it will be much easier to address than if the conflict can only be dealt with through writing, email, or the U.S. Postal Service.

Of course, there will be times when parties to a conflict refuse to communicate with each other. The facilitator of the conflict transformation may be tempted to act as a go-between. This only works to a very limited degree. I recommend limiting your efforts as a go-between to getting the parties to talk to each other. The real issues need to be expressed directly by the people involved.

Factor Five: Frame of the Conflict

The fifth factor that contributes to the context of a conflict is the "framing" of the conflict. The frame around a picture adds almost as much as the picture itself. Be aware of the frame the parties in a conflict are placing around the conflict. It may be framed as a moral conflict, a theological conflict, or just a common-sense conflict. It's sometimes important to get a new frame for the conflict to see it in a different light.

Related to the framing of the conflict is understanding what the parties really want from the conflict. More often than not, the conflict process diverts the parties from what they really want. The conflict takes on a life of its own and becomes the central issue. When this happens, the conflict develops into a matter of winning or losing rather than dealing with the issues that originally precipitated the conflict.

People get the mistaken notion they can "win" a conflict. If by winning the conflict a person means they get what they want by holding to their ground until they overpower or outlast the other party, then that's a false hope. No one can fight their way out of conflict. Think about it in terms of international conflict or a war. A country cannot fight their way out of a war; the act of fighting is the very definition of being at war. In order to end a war, those involved must at some point stop fighting long enough to come to an agreement about ending it.

Factor Six: Perception of Authority

The final factor for understanding the context of a conflict is knowing what authority someone from outside the conflict has. If someone from the outside comes with some degree of authority, either actual or perceived, it's much more likely the parties involved in the conflict will find common ground to transform the conflict into something beneficial. On the other hand, the person from outside who has little or no perceived authority may have little effect on the parties transforming the conflict.

It's incumbent on the person working with conflict to be aware of the amount of authority they carry as well as the limits of that authority. Once someone working to transform a conflict into something beneficial has their authority undermined, the conflict transformation becomes much more difficult.

The Escalating Nature of Conflict

The fact is that conflict has a life of its own. As with all living things, there's an intrinsic, motivating force which pushes a living thing toward growth. A conflict also has this seemingly intrinsic, motivating force toward growth. If left unchecked, a conflict can grow to the point where it consumes everything around it.

Conflict starts as a seed and grows to the point of full development, the final level of conflict. As with any growing thing, limiting factors can result in the growth being slowed, stunted, or stopped completely. A conflict at one level doesn't necessarily have to go to the next level. However, if a conflict is at a particular level, you can be sure that it's gone through a predictable series of escalations preceding the current level.

An observer of a conflict may not see the previous levels of a conflict. To a casual observer, the conflict may appear to have sprung fully grown into the world. Still, the early levels were there. If you ignore the early levels and focus only on the current level of a conflict, you may risk leaving the seeds in place for further destructive conflict to develop.

If you're trying to transform a conflict, it's helpful to identify where the conflict is in its growth cycle. When the current level of development is identified, appropriate interventions can be brought to bear that will aid in transforming the conflict into something useful. What follows is an examination of the levels of conflict and which factors are important to be aware of at each level. Pay attention to responses at each level that may help transform the conflict before it can advance to the next level.[8]

8   The general outline is taken from the work of Speed Leas, published in the winter 1989 issue of *Leadership Magazine*. The concept was originally developed for the article

Level One

The germination stage of conflict is where there's a problem to be solved and the people involved are committed to solving the problem. At this point, few people will recognize that there's a conflict. If the attitude of cooperation continues, there may never be what some would call conflict. Instead, something beneficial will come out of the interactions of the people involved.

At this level, most people are comfortable with conflict transformation. It's clear that the issue isn't a threat to the relationships of the people involved. If there's any intervention needed, it would be simply to affirm those involved for their commitment to relationship and to problem solving.

What's helpful is to encourage the work of transforming a level one conflict into something beneficial so the parties involved gain a sense of solidarity and accomplishment. Someone facilitating conflict transformation may be tempted to point out all the intricacies of the conflict. That tendency is best kept under control. If the level one transformation is working, the less said the better. As the old saw says, "If it ain't broke, don't fix it." Too much attention to something that's already working can cause it to go awry.

Level Two

A level two conflict develops as a level one conflict begins to run into difficulty. At first there may be a sense of general discomfort for the people involved. There's less talk about the issues involved in the problem and focus begins to shift to personal feelings about the problem itself. At this point, the people involved begin to get a

"Moving Your Church through Conflict" (Alban Institute, 1984).

sense that they might have something to lose, and as a result they begin to take steps to protect themselves.

Spotting a level two conflict isn't always easy because the people involved are trying to protect themselves. They'll be careful of what they're saying and will use a lot of generalizations. When discussing the issues involved, there will be a sense that people aren't being fully open. Things may be discussed, but significant parts of the discussion may be held back as a trump card in case things go awry.

There have been many times when people have come to me with a level two conflict. I'll hear someone say something like, "There are people who are dissatisfied with…" If I ask the person to tell me about their dissatisfaction, they'll often respond by denying any dissatisfaction, claiming that they just wanted to give me a "heads-up."

I have rarely, if ever, been called in to deal with a conflict when it's at level two. There are two primary reasons for that. The first reason is because those involved in the conflict are protecting themselves first and foremost. If an outsider is called in, the fear is that an outsider may end up being a part of an attack against those who are beginning to feel vulnerable. Secondly, when a conflict is at a level two, people seldom even realize a conflict is happening. At most they may be aware of a general sense of discomfort involving certain topics.

When I do see a level two conflict, I find it helpful to get it out into the light of day as quickly as possible. Start with the general sense of discomfort people are feeling and talk with them about what fear may be underlying their discomfort. This is one of the few times I might approach people individually rather than in a group.

Since the driving force at this level is self-protection, it may be much harder to get the parties involved to expose themselves in front of others. However, once the initial fear of exposure is overcome, it will be essential to have the whole group aware of the dynamics that are happening.

This doesn't mean I would never seek to bring things into the light in a group setting. In some situations, the level two conflict is first noticeable in a group setting. It may be that by immediately addressing the fears people have, the level two conflict can be immediately diverted into something more helpful.

The danger is that the level two conflict will continue to develop and grow. There will come a time when it shifts from being about protection and it becomes about winning. When that happens, a level three conflict is taking place.

Level Three

When a conflict has developed into a level three conflict, the parties involved have changed what they're connecting their personal identity to. In a level one conflict, identity is connected with one another or the group. The goal is to solve a problem. At level two, identity is connected with the self and protecting the self from harm. At level three, the parties involved have become identified with a particular solution. In a level one and two conflict, a particular solution is just one of many possible solutions. In level three conflicts, it's no longer a matter of one solution being one of many possible solutions, it's a matter of one solution being connected to who a person understands themself to be.

At this point, the rejection of a solution is perceived as a rejection of the individual who proposed it. The conflict has become a win-lose situation. There's little room for negotiation. Positions on issues become calcified. A person begins to believe—unconsciously, if not consciously—that they have the one true solution to the problem or the one true answer to the question. If a particular person's position isn't accepted, then *they* aren't accepted. Being "right" is an absolute.

There's also a shift in how people present the issue. The generalities which appear in level two are modified. Instead of "some people are dissatisfied," it becomes "everyone is dissatisfied." The person who makes this shift is now trying to build a cohort of likeminded people as a way of bolstering their position.

There may still be a lack of clarity about the source of the dissatisfaction. In addition to the lack of clarity, there may be outright distortion of information. A claim by one person that they'll quit a particular committee in a church if things don't go their way may be distorted into "half the church is planning on leaving and going their own way."

At this point, there will be the preliminary development of factions. These aren't full-blown alliances, but groupings of people who "think the same way." What's happening is that people are seeking safety. There will be fear that they will be marginalized or totally cast aside. The conflict is now moving closer to being a matter of survival.

The facilitator at this stage will do their best to create a safe environment for everyone to be heard. It's important to clarify any misstatements and to get specificity where there are generalizations. However, it's also important to realize that the clarifications are best if they come from the parties involved in the conflict rather than some authority. If, for example, a pastor or an outside facilitator attempts to point out the generalizations and distortions, one or more of the parties involved may see that as joining with the other side.

At this level of conflict, an outside facilitator will be a new factor in the equation. People may be willing to hear someone who doesn't have a stake in the conflict. The outside facilitator is less likely to be seen as supporting one side or another, at least initially.

There is a danger for the person being brought in from outside. It's tempting for the outside facilitator to see themself as the "white knight riding to the rescue." If that happens, it's likely that everyone involved in the conflict will see that person as an intruder and the outsider may lose whatever authority they brought into the situation. The parties involved will do best if they find their own clarification and solutions to the issues. The outside facilitator should primarily help the opposing parties discover what they know and are willing to do.

Once a level three win-lose situation has developed, quick action is essential. If something doesn't change, then the next level, in theological terms, is a schism.

Level Four

A schism is a separation, a cutting asunder of something that had been a whole. In everyday terms, it's a divorce. Winning and losing are no longer important. What's important is to get rid of the "troublemaker," who is by definition on the "other side" of the issue.

Developmentally, people have come to the point of being so identified with their position on the issue or issues involved that they see any opposition as threatening everything they believe about themselves. They not only identify with the issue, in effect they *become* the issue. Words are no longer enough, action is required. The parties involved come to believe the only action that will provide safety is total separation from those who disagree.

At this level, there are clear factions involved. There are usually leaders who can be identified and who either act as a spokesperson for their faction or who direct the words of whoever is the spokesperson. In a church setting, there will be political maneuvers to "get rid" of the other side. At times, this is an attempt at complete marginalization, rendering the other side totally impotent. Usually, it's a desire to get the other side to leave.

Like many divorces, conflict at this level can become very dirty. Anything and everything can become fair game in order to accomplish the task of "purifying" the group and establishing a person's own position as the only right position.

At this point, it's nearly impossible for anyone who has ties to any of the parties involved to be effective. In a church setting, a pastor who tries to intervene when conflict has reached level four may well find that all of the parties involved will turn against them and unite with each other in opposition to the pastor. In these cases, an outside facilitator is required. What may be needed is a conflict specialist, a Transitional Pastor, an Intentional Interim Pastor, a denominational leader, or a trusted pastor or lay leader from another church. In any case, the person who's called in will need to have significant skill in conflict transformation.

The goal now becomes reawakening the connections which originally bound the parties together. It may or may not be necessary to look at the process by which the current state of affairs came to be. The conflict has now reached a point where a misstep could result in death, figuratively, if not literally. The opposing parties are at a point where they'll either find some common ground or they'll completely sever their relationship.

Level Five

At level five, the parties involved have decided that not only is winning and losing not enough, not only is total separation not enough, but death for the opposing parties is the only acceptable solution. It may be a real death or a symbolic death, but death nonetheless. The conflict has escalated into a holy war. To give in or to appear to walk away in any way is to deny one's faith.

If the conflict is between a pastor and a congregation, the congregation may not only want the pastor fired, but perhaps legally prosecuted or sued in civil court. The congregation may go to great lengths to let other congregations know how "evil" the pastor is and seek to keep him from serving any church ever again. I've seen cases where a congregation even sought to keep a former pastor from getting a secular job in another state.

It should be noted that pastors who are personally a part of conflict at this level will also be involved in the holy war syndrome. It becomes their solemn obligation to see that the congregation is never served by another competent pastor. The pastor may initiate a law suit or spread rumors in the community intended to destroy the congregation. The only way the pastor will ever feel satisfied is if the church closes its doors forever.

At this stage, the facilitator may only be facilitating a separation which keeps the parties from each other's throats. A change at this point has a clear name associated with it: it's called a "miracle." Miracles do happen. However, they're the exception and not the rule.

Mixed-Level Conflicts

All parties to a conflict may not be at the same level. One party may be at level one and another may be at level two. In this case, one party believes the problem is still something that can be worked out and is still committed to finding a solution. The other party, however, has begun to fear they can't protect themselves and have begun moving toward generalization in order to make their point.

I've seen several cases where the parties are at different levels, but I don't recall any case where the difference in level was more than a single level. One party may be at level two and another at level three, but never have I seen a case where one party was at level two and the other party was at level four. The reason for this is that conflict is about survival. When the stakes are increased by one party, the other party will have to increase the stakes or surrender the field.

It's important to not only be aware of the levels of conflict in general, but to be able to understand what level each individual party is at. It's also important to understand what contributes to movement to the next level. A skilled facilitator will be aware of the difference and be aware of what interventions are needed with each party.

Approaches to Conflict

Fight or Flight

A long-established psychological principle is the fight or flight reflex. When faced with conflict, the parties involved have a common goal of being conflict free. They will attempt to accomplish this goal by running away (flight) or using force to overpower the other party (fight).

If both parties use the flight approach, the result will most likely be a submerged conflict. Submerged conflicts can continue for years. Neither party will really examine the conflict. Instead of the conflict being transformed into something beneficial, it will fester and continue to drain power from both parties.

On the other hand, if both parties try to use force—physical, emotional, or political—to gain what they want, a very hot conflict can emerge. A hot conflict not only drains the resources of those involved, but it may also produce collateral damage. Parties not actually involved in the conflict may be drawn in.

Of course, there may be a situation where one party chooses the fight response and the other party chooses the flight response. This doesn't mean the group that chooses to fight wins. What it means is that one side will be obvious and open in its attack on the issues of the other side, and the other party may well be constantly attacking in a passive aggressive fashion. This keeps the conflict from being clearly seen and therefore makes it impossible to transform.

It's been my experience with churches that the flight response predominates. The passive aggressive response is more the rule than the exception. This may be because churches have an inaccurate view of conflict. Christians believe they should "love one another" and that loving one another means "not fighting." They will therefore avoid a direct confrontation of the issue.

This head-in-the-sand approach seldom ends a conflict. Instead, it can result in a nasty, submarine-type warfare, where one side constantly torpedoes the other side and the other side is constantly being surprised that their goals, which aren't openly opposed, are thwarted. Such conflicts can go on for years in a church resulting in the church being ineffective in ministry.

Dialogue

It should be obvious by now that dialogue is a major part of conflict transformation. Dialogue between the various parties must be established in order for there to be a transformation of the conflict. Dialogue means a true give and take and exchange of ideas, wants, needs, and hopes. Dialogue involves more than just talking. Dialogue means really been able to hear and understand what the other person is saying as well as being able to communicate one's own position.

Here are some guidelines for establishing a dialogue between parties in conflict: First, the elements of good communication must be established. The parties have to come to some form of agreement as to what they will and will not do in the dialogue process. Some of the obvious rules are things such as no name-calling and no putdowns. Generally speaking, good dialogue is about good communication techniques. Don't assume that adults will know how to communicate and carry on dialogue. A common misconception is that dialogue is simply talking. This can result in a lot of talking and very little listening.

A second rule of establishing dialogue is that it's best accomplished in an atmosphere where there are no interruptions. This may mean during the conflict transformation process it will be necessary to go to a location where the parties won't be interrupted in any way. It may mean turning off cell phones, leaving computers and e-mail behind, and putting a "DO NOT DISTURB" sign on the door.

Third, dialogue must remain focused on the issues. This is often the hardest part of the dialogue. I've seen conflict situations where the initial conflict issue was pretty clear and direct. However, as the conversation continued, the parties involved brought up peripheral topics that weren't directly related to the original issue. The conflict issue becomes less clear and the focus became very diffuse.

Fourth, remember that a helpful dialogue isn't likely to happen quickly. It will take time to develop. The dialogue that's needed for conflict transformation will have to mature. The dialogue may start out on a rather juvenile level, and transformation won't take place until it reaches a mature level.

There are two corollaries to the idea that dialogue takes time to develop. Corollary one: The facilitator and the parties involved have to approach the dialogue with a lot of patience. It's wise to assume that more time will be needed for the dialogue to take place than you might guess. Corollary two: If the parties aren't willing to commit time to the dialogue, transformation is unlikely to take place.

Finally, when two or more parties are involved in a conflict, dialogue is usually best achieved when it's facilitated by a non-involved third party. Once a conflict gets rolling, it's hard for the parties involved to maintain objectivity. The responsibilities of this non-involved third party are to listen carefully to the words that are spoken, identify the frame that's being put on the conflict, and help the parties involved to identify internal issues that may be driving the conflict.

Unhelpful Approaches to Conflict

Conflict is something we deal with all the time. That doesn't mean we deal with it in a way which can transform it into something beneficial. There are some approaches which are either not helpful or are actually counterproductive. These have been touched on in previous discussions, but it's helpful to single them out so they'll be clearly in mind.

A common way of dealing with conflict is to deny that there is any conflict. We seem to function under the illusion that if we don't talk about it, it doesn't exist. Parties in conflict can greet each other as if they were long-lost friends while watching for a way to stab the other person in the back. If asked about conflict, both may vehemently deny there's any such thing. The bottom line is that denial of conflict leads to submarine warfare.

Another very common approach to dealing with conflict is the use of force. The force doesn't have to be physical. Shouting is a form of force. Some people resort to using emotional force. Any action in which one party seeks to compel another party into an agreement is most likely a situation where force is being used.

In most church conflict situations, force is rarely physical, although I was in one church situation which came to physical blows. This was a situation between a man and woman who were both leaders. The man was using force through name calling ("You are a Jezebel"); the woman became frustrated and slapped him. The conflict remained unresolved.

Facilitators may also try to use force to bring about a resolution to the conflict. It may be through the force of their authority or the use of some other threat. It isn't unusual to resort to calling on God as the force to judge the other party or parties.

It's rare that force alone will be enough to transform a conflict into something beneficial. If the facilitator succeeds in getting what appears to be a resolution, it's likely the resolution will last only as long as the parties involved perceive the facilitator as having the power to use force.

Even using force simply to get parties to sit down to dialogue may be counterproductive. The use of force may set up a conflict between the parties and the facilitator. Someone once said to me, "Anything that is pushed will push back." The very use of force may increase a conflict.

Another ineffective way of dealing with conflict is withdrawal. In the case of withdrawal, one party or the other simply walks away from the battle. While this appears to bring the conflict to an end, there's been no transformation of the conflict into something beneficial to all the parties involved. In addition, it's likely that the party which walked away will walk away with feelings of hurt, helplessness, and resentment. The party which appears to have won the conflict will walk away with a false sense of victory.

There are long-term implications for the use of withdrawal in conflict situations. In the future, the withdrawing party will most likely withdraw again and again, resulting in a loss of their identity. On the other hand, the party that appears to have won won't have learned how to move beyond conflict to transform it into something beneficial.

The flip side of withdrawal from conflict situations is exclusion. In this case, one party has enough power to simply exclude the party they're in conflict with. While this may appear to end a conflict, it will most likely push the excluded party into a submarine warfare. The only way to avoid submarine warfare will be for the excluding party to completely cut off the excluded party. The most extreme physical form of exclusion is murder.

The final counterproductive approach to conflict is advice-giving or advice-seeking. Advice that is given, whether offered or asked for, will rarely solve the issues that produced a conflict in the first place. That's because the issues of the conflict aren't usually what they appear to be.

It isn't unusual in my experience to have someone say, "You're the expert, what do you think we should do?" When I hear that, I assume one of two things. One, the party asking doesn't really want to end the conflict, but wants to look like they're attempting to deal with it. Or, two, the party asking is trying to flatter me so I'll join their side.

Novices to conflict transformation are often seduced by one or both parties attempting to get the facilitator to offer their wisdom about the situation. When advice is given, the parties involved are cheated of the opportunity to learn how to resolve their own conflicts in the future. In addition, the facilitator who gives advice is likely to lose objectivity if their advice is rejected. If the advice is accepted, and doesn't work, then the facilitator will appear ineffective to the parties involved and, perhaps more importantly, to themself.

Concluding Thoughts

I ENJOY TRANSITIONAL MINISTRY. More specifically, I enjoy Intentional Interim Ministry or Transitional Ministry. I like that I have a clear goal in mind when I begin and that there will come a time when it's clear my work is at an end. I have an opportunity to make a difference with a congregation that is psychologically ready for change.

There are disadvantages to doing this kind of ministry, of course. I'm always saying goodbye to people. Just when I really get to know and appreciate them, they become part of my past. I'll also have periods of time where I'm unable to do the actual work. The ending of my work at one church doesn't always coincide with another congregation deciding it would benefit from an Intentional Interim Pastor or a Transitional Pastor. That could mean a gap of a few weeks or a gap of several months.

However, it's a blessing to serve God in transitional ministry work. It's a position where you can look forward to what God will do in the future. It's a position where you can be challenged to grow psychologically and more importantly, spiritually.

Appendix A:
Sample Contracts

Here are four sample contracts or memorandums of understanding between a transitional (interim) pastor and a particular congregation. The exact format will vary from denomination to denomination. In some cases, a regional or denominational representative is expected to be a witness to the agreement.

Note that these four examples are only examples and each will need to be modified to meet the needs of a particular transitional pastor and a particular congregation. The final contract, letter of understanding, or covenant should be the result of negotiations between the congregation and the transitional pastor.

Model for a Transitional Pastor Job Description

These are general guidelines and expectations. Many of the following responsibilities will depend on the amount of time each week the Transitional Pastor spends with you. Unless the Transitional Pastor is called full time, the church should expect that pastoral care will be less than that of a permanent pastor. A specific covenant should be established between the church board and the Transitional Pastor (see template below for a guideline).

The Transitional Pastor will be responsible for:

1. Preaching and leading the worship life of the congregation, including Sunday worship services.
2. Leading other services as needed and agreed upon with the congregation. (Specify.)
3. Provide opportunities for members of the congregation to talk about their feelings, hurts, and hopes surrounding the resignation of their previous pastor. Assist the congregation in proceeding through any grief, anger, or health issues in readiness to embrace new pastoral leadership.

4. Adhere to the "Covenant and Code of Ethics" for Professional Church leaders, and the "Transitional Pastors _(denomination)_ Code of Ethics."

5. Officiate at baptisms, weddings, and funerals as requested, and lead baptismal and membership classes as needed.

6. Visit the sick and shut-ins and counsel members as requested. In the case of a part-time Transitional Pastor, this responsibility should be handled by the appropriate board or team of the church that handles member care.

7. Attend and provide guidance at appropriate meetings of official boards and committees.

8. Work with the Consultant for Transitioning Ministry and the congregational leadership to provide the most effective transition ministry for the congregation. Work with the leadership in addressing the results of the assessment(s), and in exploring ways in which the church can become more Missional in their focus.

9. Provide education to the congregation on what it means to be a Missional church.

10. Assist the congregation in maintaining, establishing, or reconnecting ties with the Region.

11. At no time will the Transitional Pastor be considered a candidate for any staff position in the congregation with which they serve, unless indicated otherwise by the Consultant for Transitioning Ministry.

12. Participate in an evaluation of the transition period. A form is provided to the church leadership to be completed

and returned to the Consultant for Transitioning Ministry.

13. Provide effective closure when it is time to leave. This would also include preparing the congregation for supporting new pastoral leadership.

TRANSITIONAL PASTOR/CHURCH AGREEMENT

Entered into this _____ day of _____, 20_____ by Reverend _(name of pastor)_ **("Minister") and the** _(name of church)_ **("church") for the employment of the minister effective_____, 20___. THE** _(name of church)_ **AGREES:**

1. To provide a total (weekly, daily, units) compensation package of $_____ as remuneration for the time agreed upon below.

2. Additional time requested by the church will either be compensated at the rate of $_____ per _____, or comp time given. Any such agreement must be understood and communicated in writing between _(name of pastor)_ and the _(name of board or chairperson)_.

3. To provide reimbursement for professional expenses incurred by the Transitional Pastor as a result of performing ministerial duties, not to exceed $_____ per month. In addition, ____ days per quarter for professional development related to Transitional Ministry.

4. To provide reimbursement for mileage incurred in pastoral calling and one round trip from home per week, at *(the current IRS rate)* .

5. To provide paid vacation as follows:_____
_____ (we recommend one week for every three months of service completed)

6. To provide overnight accommodations when distance of travel to and from home makes a daily round trip unreasonable, and when weather or ministry requires such.

7. To conduct a monthly review of the pastor-church relationship focusing on the criteria established in the Transitional Pastor's job description.

THE TRANSITIONAL PASTOR AGREES:

8. To sign and adhere to "The Transitional Pastors *(denomination)* Code of Ethics" and "The Covenant and Code of Ethics for Professional Church Leaders of *(denomination)* ."

9. To carefully review and adhere to the Job Description for the Transitional Pastor.

10. To provide a monthly written report to the *(name of appropriate church official)* .

11. To keep within the expense account and submit a monthly report of expenses to the *(name of appropriate church official)* .

12. To be available on specified days of the week, in addition to Sunday, and will hold the following regular office hours: _(specify hours)_ .

13. This agreement will be effective for _(6, 9, 12 months, etc.)_ from date of signing below, and can be cancelled or renegotiated with thirty days written notice by either party.

Both parties have received, read, and mutually agree to the above.

Date: _____   _____ _(name of church)_ _____

       BY: _____ _(signature of appropriate church official)_ _____
       AS ITS _____ _(name of church office)_ _____

Date: _____

       BY: _____ _(signature of Transitional Pastor)_ _____

Suggested Compensation:

We recommend the following guidelines for compensation:

"Salary"

$200-250 per day, based on the experience of the Transitional Pastor and the needs of the church. Sunday would be considered one day. You may also negotiate compensation based on number of units per week (a unit being a 3-4 hour block of time, at $100-150 per unit).

Mileage

Regular compensation:

1. One round trip per week for those who travel a distance, at the current IRS rate.
2. Additional mileage, at the IRS rate, for a round trip when transitional pastor is called to be present in a crisis situation.
3. Additional mileage, at the IRS rate, for ministry-related travel.

Ministry-Related Expenses

Reimbursement for ministry-related expenses, and reasonable compensated time, for professional development related to the responsibilities of the Transitional Pastor (training, seminars, workshops, clergy retreat, etc).

Other Compensation

No other benefits are normally offered, however they can be negotiated. (Retirement, health benefits, social security offset.)

If the transitional minister owns their home, they may request the compensation be given as housing allowance and reported on the W-2. To satisfy IRS regulations, this agreement must be in writing, must be noted in the church minutes, and may not be more than the actual cost of the expenses the Transitional Pastor incurs in owning or renting a home (including utilities). It is the responsibility of the Transitional Pastor, rather than the church, to justify such amounts to the IRS.

EXAMPLE 2:
Model for an Interim Ministry Covenant-Contract

INTERIM (TRANSITIONAL) MINISTRY COVENANT-CONTRACT

between

(name of church) Church and The Reverend *(name of pastor)*

For the purpose of providing interim pastoral leadership during a period of rediscovery and adjustment to change, it is agreed that the Rev. *(name of pastor)* will begin service as Interim (Transitional) Pastor of *(name of church)* Church, *(community)* , *(state)*, on *(date)* .

It is understood that this Covenant-Contract will be reviewed at least every six months. During this period, the Interim (Transitional) pastor and congregation will, in covenant with one another and with the help of God, seek to:

* provide worship experiences and the practice of ministry with the congregation and community;

* engage in congregational self-study and goal setting by reviewing the past and planning for the future in such a way as to strengthen and enhance the mission and unity of *(name of church)* Church;

* prepare for the ministry of a pastor who will be duly called by the congregation.

It is further agreed that the Interim (Transitional) Pastor will not meet with the pastoral search committee or assist in the selection of a pastoral candidate. It may be helpful, at times, to advise the committee in terms of process, but this may be done only in consultation with and agreement of the Conference staff person resourcing the search process and the chair of the search committee.

It is understood that under no circumstances may the Interim (Transitional) Pastor be a candidate for the position of called pastor. For *(denomination)* clergy, such violations could result in a loss of ministerial standing. For clergy of other denominations, violations could result in a denial of ministerial standing.

OUR SHARED EXPECTATIONS:

The pastoral and professional leadership provided by The Rev. *(name of pastor)* will amount to *(full, 3/4, 1/2, or 1/4)* time per week. Should additional time be needed to   provide   pastoral services, the matter will be reviewed by the *(name of appropriate board/committee)* ; and either the members of the church will assist with the pastoral duties or additional compensation will be offered to the Interim (Transitional) Pastor.

[THE FOLLOWING IS A POSSIBLE LIST OF SOME OF THE PASTORAL RESPONSIBILITIES FOR A FULL-TIME INTERIM (TRANSITIONAL)

PASTOR; PART-TIME SERVICE IS ADJUSTED ACCORDINGLY.]

Pastoral services requested include:

1. Leadership of Sunday worship, administration of the sacraments, and special services as needed.
2. Counseling and/or referral in crisis situations.
3. Serving as lead teacher and resource for the Confirmation program.
4. Visitation of hospitalized and shut-in members, as well as other pastoral calls.
5. Providing pastoral services for weddings and funerals.
6. Attending and resourcing meeting of the boards/committees of the church each month, plus other groups as requested.
7. Providing leadership for adult education/Bible study groups.
8. Providing leadership and training for members in the special emphases of the church, including congregational self-study, future planning, membership outreach, and stewardship.
9. Providing administrative oversight for the daily affairs of the church, including being "head of staff."
10. Remaining active in the _(name of church)_ in the _(name of association)_ and the _(name of regional denominational offices)_.

The Interim pastor will be responsible to the congregation at large, and specifically to the _(responsible board or committee within the church)_ .

The congregation will support and cooperate with the Interim (Transitional) Pastor in every way and will assume responsibility for:

1. attendance at worship and meetings;
2. continued financial support for the church and its mission and ministries;
3. support of the Interim pastor in the ministry of the church to the community;
4. sustained lay leadership and shared ministry;
5. the establishment of an Interim Ministry Committee of not more than five persons agreed upon by the Interim (Transitional) Pastor and the governing board of the church whose purpose will be to serve as a confidential support and advising group for the Interim Pastor, to monitor the progress of the accomplishment of Interim Tasks, and to act as a communication link between the Interim (Transitional) Pastor and the congregation;
6. participation in the Association and Denominational affairs;
7. secretarial support services;
8. financial support and time for the Interim Pastor to engage in continuing education opportunities (guideline is one day for each month of service).

It is agreed that this covenant-contract shall be in effect for twelve months or until sixty days following the extension of a call to a new pastor, whichever comes first, after which time it can be extended up to the time of the start-up of the new pastor. However, _____ months shall be considered maximum time for the interim (transitional) period. Thirty-days' notice shall be given in writing by either party of intention to decline an extension.

Because the particular tasks of the interim period need the better part of a year to accomplish, should the congregation wish to terminate the services of the Interim Pastor prior to the calling of a pastor, ninety days written notice shall be given and the congregation shall be responsible for maintaining the Interim (Transitional) Pastor's regular compensation package, including accumulated vacation and continuing education time for a total of eleven months from the time of the beginning of this contract. If the Interim (Transitional) Pastor should wish to terminate this contract prior to the calling of a new pastor, sixty days written notice shall be given.

COMPENSATION

For pastoral services rendered as outlined above, it is agreed that The Rev. _(name of pastor)_ shall receive the following by way of compensation:

(GUIDELINE: A full-time Interim Pastor should receive either the same compensation package as the previous pastor or that being offered to the incoming pastor, whichever is greater.)

    SALARY: $ _____ per month

    HOUSING: $ _____ per month

AUTO/TRAVEL REIMBURSEMENT: *(the current IRS rate)* .

CONTINUING EDUCATION ALLOWANCE: $_____ for _____ months.

FULL PREMIUM PAYMENTS for appropriate denominational annuity, group life, health, dental, and disability plans.

VACATION with pay accumulating to $_____ for each _____ of pastoral service, or four weeks if a year's interim (transitional) ministry is served. Unless otherwise stated herein, some or all of the earned vacation may be taken at the conclusion of the Interim Pastor's term of service to the congregation, as long as it is prior to the start-up of the new pastor.

MOVING EXPENSES as necessary, or if the Interim Pastor lives within commuting distance of his/her residence, a mileage reimbursement for the commute of not less than *(the current IRS rate)* per mile.

DISABILITY - In the case of disability because of accident or illness, the church shall be responsible for the Interim Pastor's full salary for the first three months of disability, which includes base salary, housing, the average of travel reimbursement, payment of the congregation's share of the Family Protection Plan, annuity payments, and health insurance. After three months, the Family Protection Plan becomes effective. This agreement shall be in effect by mutual consent of the governing body of the church, the Interim Pastor, and/or his/her family, the Conference Minister and/or the Association Committee on Church and Ministry.

DEATH - In the case of the Interim Pastor's death prior to a period of disability, the spouse and/or family shall receive full salary and housing for three months, plus any earned vacation pay.

SABBATICAL LEAVE AND EMERGENCY FUND - It is strongly recommended to all congregations served by a trained Interim Ministry Specialist that it contribute a minimum of $50.00 per month of service to a "Sabbatical Leave and Emergency Fund" to be held in escrow and made available to the Interim Pastor upon request.

In accepting this agreement, effective *(date)*, we hereby attach our signatures, making this covenant-contract binding upon us in accordance with the above outlined terms.

Interim (Transitional) Pastor: *(signature of Transitional Pastor)*

Date: _____

For the Church: _____ *(name of church)* _____

Office Held: _____ *(name of church office)* _____

Date: _____

Conference Staff: _____

Date: _____

For the Association's Church and Ministry Committee:

_____

Date: _____

EXAMPLE 3:
Model for an Interim Ministry Covenant Agreement

Covenant Agreement between

Rev. _(name of pastor)_ and _(name of church)_ Church

This covenant between the Rev. _(name of pastor)_ who holds standing in _(denominational affiliation)_, and _(name of church)_ Church, of (city, State, is effective beginning _(date)_.

Responsibilities and Duties

The Interim (Transitional) Pastor shall:

1. Intentionally lead the congregation through the congregation's Developmental Tasks:
   A. Coming to terms with the congregation's history.
   B. Discerning the congregation's purpose and identity.
   C. Supporting leadership change and development.
   D. Reaffirming and strengthening denominational links.
   E. Committing to new leadership and new ministry.

2. Fulfill the normal duties of a pastor including:
   A. Lead and preach in the congregation's worship services.

B. Administer church business and oversee the church staff.

C. Work with the congregation's governing body and its program committees.

D. Oversee the preparation of worship bulletin and newsletter.

E. Visit members who are hospitalized, homebound, and nursing facility residents.

F. Conduct funerals for members and friends of the congregation.

G. Officiate at weddings for members and friends of the congregation.

H. Provide counseling and make appropriate referrals.

I. Teach confirmation/new member class for youths and adults.

J. Maintain a collegial relationship with the area clergy association.

K. Provide counsel to the pastoral search committee when requested and focused only upon the process, not upon potential pastors.

The congregation shall:

1. Commit to the process of self-study by working through the Developmental Tasks.

2. Seriously consider implementing programs suggested by the (*name of pastor*).

3. Establish goals prior to each evaluation period.

4. Actively pursue the calling of a settled pastor.

5. Function as the "Body of Christ," making visits to worship guests, members in hospitals, nursing facilities, homebound, and inactive members.

6. Maintain education, mission, music, and other ministries of the congregation.

7. Continue to provide staff support.

8. Support the involvement of the Interim Pastor in denominational activities, clergy associations, and Interim Ministers' support groups.

9. Provide resources for professional consultation with specialists, when needed, in order to assist the Interim (Transitional) Pastor in accomplishing the goals of interim (transitional) ministry.

10. Establish an interim (transitional) ministry/transitional team (pastoral relations committee or other group) to serve as a confidential support and advisory group for the Interim (Transitional) Pastor, to monitor progress in accomplishing the Developmental Tasks and to act as a link between the pastor and the congregation.

Accountability

The Interim Pastor shall:

1. Be accountable to the council through the executive council and ultimately to the congregation for the successful completion of duties.

2. Maintain ministerial standing in his denomination.

3. Maintain contact with his Association and home congregation.

The congregation shall:

1. Support the leadership of the Interim Pastor in the congregation and community.

2. Inform the Interim (Transitional) Pastor regularly of the progress the pastoral search committee is making in preparing to call a settled pastor.

Salary and Benefits

For all services rendered by the interim pastor under this agreement, _(name of church)_ agrees to provide the following annual compensation:

$ _____ Cash salary _(frequency of payment)_

$ _____ Housing allowance

$ _____ Use of parsonage with all utilities*

$ _____ Pension

$ _____ Life Insurance and Disability Income Plan

$ _____ Social Security Offset (7.65% of salary basis)

$ _____ Health Insurance

$ _____ Dental Insurance

Parsonage is valued at 130% of cash salary for purpose of calculating "salary basis" to determine benefits.

Reimbursable Professional Expenses

$ _____ Continuing Education

$ _____ Professional expenses (meetings, etc.)

$ _____ Mileage to be reimbursed at _(the current IRS rate)_

$ _____ Other (telephone, etc.)

Compensation shall be reviewed and determined annually.

The congregation shall pay moving expenses as necessary and appropriate.

Paid vacation: one week for each 3 months of service, or 2½ days per month served.

NOTE: When an Interim Pastor is serving a great distance from his/her home, negotiation of "family time," in addition to vacation time, is encouraged.

One week of Continuing Education time for each 6 months of service.

Due to the itinerant nature of interim (transitional) ministry, if the Interim (Transitional) Pastor does not have a call at the completion of the interim, he/she may wish to negotiate a severance equal to one month's income (numbers 1-6 above).

Review and Evaluation

There shall be regular three-month reviews of the mutual ministry of the congregation and the interim pastor. Those participating in the review may include the _(name of church)_ administrative body, chairs of committees, and the Interim (Transitional) Pastor. The purposes are to:

- Determine progress on goals;

- Provide the interim pastor and congregational representatives an opportunity to assess how well they are fulfilling responsibilities and the ministries they share;

- Identify and isolate any areas of conflict or disappointment that have not received adequate attention and may be adversely affecting mutual ministry;

- Clarify expectations of all parties to help avoid or to deal with any possible future conflicts.

A mutually-agreed-upon third party (denominational staff or designee) may be engaged to facilitate the ministry review process.

Exit Interview

At the conclusion of the interim relationship, the local church and pastor agree to participate in an evaluation of the interim (transitional) period. This evaluation would typically include the following:

1. An exit interview attended by the Interim (Transitional) Pastor and key lay leaders; and
2. Completion of evaluation process suggested by the denominational staff.

Duration, Renewal, and Termination

This covenant is initially in effect for six months and is renewable in three-month increments, as appropriate and agreeable to both parties, following evaluation.

Either party may terminate this agreement with a thirty (30) day notice. Changes in the above covenant may be negotiated between the Interim (Transitional) Pastor and the executive council of the congregation.

Non-Candidacy Covenant

The Interim Pastor agrees to the following covenant: *"Under no circumstances will I allow my name to be considered as a possible candidate for the settled position."* Likewise the church agrees that the Interim (Transitional) Pastor will not be considered as a possible candidate for the settled position.

In accepting this agreement, effective _(date)_ , we hereby attach our signatures, making the covenant binding upon us in accordance with the above outlined terms, subject to the approval of the governing board on _(date)_ .

Interim Pastor   *Date*

Congregational Representative   *Date*

Association/ Regional Representative   *Date*

Suggestions for goals for the first quarter:

- Establish a working relationship with teams and committees.

- Review staff contracts, required evaluations, and establish working relationship with staff.

- Establish office hours, invite members and groups to share their stories with pastor and with each other.

- Demonstrate adequate time and thought was invested in worship planning and presentation.

- Establish connections with local partners in ministry.

EXAMPLE 4:
Model for an Interim Ministry Covenant

INTERIM MINISTRY COVENANT

This covenant with _(name of pastor)_ who holds standing in _(denominational affiliation)_ is effective beginning _(date)_ .

Responsibilities and Duties

The Interim Pastor shall:

1. Intentionally lead the congregation through prayerful discernment of the congregation's Developmental Focus Points of: Heritage, Leadership, Mission, Connection, and Future.

2. Upon arrival, the Interim Pastor will work with the church council to establish:

   A. **Shared Outcomes** for the Interim Process that will be used to guide the process and as a basis of evaluation for the process;

   B. **A Transition Team** to work with the Interim in guiding the discernment of the Developmental Focus Points and achieving the Shared Outcomes for the interim process.

3. Fulfill the normal duties of a pastor, including:

   A. Lead and preach in the congregation's worship services.

   B. Administer church business and oversee the church staff.

   C. Work with the congregation's governing body and its program committees.

   D. Oversee the preparation of worship bulletin and newsletter.

   E. Visit members who are hospitalized, homebound, and nursing facility residents.

   F. Conduct funerals for members and friends of the congregation.

   G. Officiate at weddings for members and friends of the congregation.

   H. Provide counseling and make appropriate referrals.

   I. Teach confirmation/new member class for youths and adults.

   J. Maintain a collegial relationship with the area clergy association.

   K. Provide counsel to the pastoral search committee when requested and focused only upon the process, not upon potential pastors.

The congregation shall:

1. Commit to the process of self-study by working through the Focus Points.

2. Seriously consider implementing programs suggested by the Interim Pastor.
3. Actively pursue the calling of a settled pastor.
4. Function as the "Body of Christ," making visits to worship guests, members in hospitals, nursing
5. facilities, homebound, and inactive members.
6. Maintain education, mission, music, and other ministries of the congregation.
7. Continue to provide staff support.
8. Support the involvement of the Interim Pastor in denominational activities, clergy associations, and Interim Ministers' support groups.
9. Provide resources for professional consultation with specialists, when needed, in order to assist the Interim Pastor in accomplishing the goals of interim ministry.
10. Establish an interim ministry/transition team and a pastor relations committee to serve as a confidential support and advisory group for the interim pastor, to monitor progress in accomplishing the developmental tasks and to act as a link between the pastor and congregation.

Accountability

The Interim Pastor shall:

1. Be accountable to the council and ultimately to the congregation for the successful completion of duties.
2. Maintain ministerial standing in his denomination.

3. Maintain contact with his Association and home congregation.

The congregation shall:

1. Support the leadership of the Interim Pastor in the congregation and community.
2. Inform the Interim Pastor regularly of the progress the pastoral search committee is making in preparing to call a settled pastor.

Salary and Benefits

For all services rendered by the Interim Pastor under this agreement, the _(name of church and affiliation_)of _(city)_ , _(state)_ , agrees to provide the following annual compensation:

$ _____Cash salary (pay periods are weekly, starting one week after service begins)

$ _____Housing allowance (the church will carry the lease)

$ _____Pension (14% of salary basis, i.e., cash salary + housing allowance)

$ _____Life Insurance and Disability Income Plan (1.5% of salary basis)

$ _____Social Security Offset (7.65% of salary basis)

$ _____Health Insurance

$ _____Health Insurance

$ _____Health Insurance

$ _____Dental Insurance

$ _____Vision Insurance to start _(date)_

Reimbursable Professional Expenses

Continuing Education

Professional expenses

Mileage to be reimbursed at _(the current IRS rate)_

Other (telephone, etc.)

Compensation shall be reviewed and determined annually.

The congregation shall pay moving expenses as necessary and appropriate.

Paid vacation: one week for each three (3) months of service or two (2) days per month served.

One week of continuing education time for six (6) months of service.

Review and Evaluation

There shall be regular six-month reviews of the mutual ministry of the congregation and the Interim Pastor. Those participating in the review may include the _(named church administrative body)_, chairs of committees, and the interim pastor. The purposes are to:

- Determine progress on goals;

- Provide the interim pastor and congregational representatives an opportunity to assess how well they are fulfilling responsibilities and the ministries they share;

- Identify and isolate any areas of conflict or disappointment that have not received adequate attention and may be adversely affecting mutual ministry;

- Clarify expectations of all parties to help avoid or to deal with any possible future conflicts.

- A mutually agreed upon third party (Conference staff or designee) may be engaged to facilitate the ministry review process.

Exit Interview

At the conclusion of the interim relationship, the local church and pastor agree to participate in an evaluation of the interim period. This evaluation would typically include the following:

- An exit interview attended by the Interim (Transitional) Pastor and key lay leaders; and

- Completion of evaluation process suggested by the denominational staff;

- Duration, renewal, and termination.

This covenant is initially in effect for twelve months and is renewable in twelve-month increments, as appropriate and agreeable to both parties, following evaluation.

When both **the congregation** and **the Intentional Interim (the "Interim")** *jointly agree* they have satisfied the work the congregation set out to accomplish (see Outcomes), either party may formally give **NINETY (90) day notice** in writing, by certified mail or personal delivery; the congregation gives notice through action taken by the governing board and noted in minutes. In such case, the congregation will be responsible for maintaining the Interim's compensation through the actual time of service and the congregation also agrees to the continuation of compensation as described below:

- Recognizing the unique challenges Interims face in frequent transition, the congregation agrees that the Interim will continue to receive all compensation for up to a period of ninety (90) days after termination or until the Interim has secured and has begun functioning in a new call;

- The maximum time after termination that the Interim will receive such compensation shall be ninety (90) days.

- It is the intention of both parties to make reasonable efforts to discuss, prevent, and resolve any misunderstandings, including initiating help from denominational or other outside expertise, to avoid cancellation of this agreement.

- However, should the congregation wish to unilaterally terminate the agreement prior to the call of a new settled pastor and acceptance by same, with or without joint consultation with the Interim, no more than THIRTY

(30) days' notice in writing shall be given, by certified mail or personal delivery, including action taken by the governing board and noted in minutes; less by mutual consent. In such case, the congregation will be responsible for maintaining the Interim's compensation through the initially intended date of the agreement's termination, but not less than SIX (6) months.

- Should the Interim unilaterally terminate the agreement prior to the call of a new settled pastor and acceptance by same, with or without joint consultation with the congregation, no more than THIRTY (30) days' notice in writing shall be given, by certified mail or personal delivery, including action taken by the governing board and noted in minutes; less by mutual consent. In such case, the congregation will be responsible for maintaining the Interim's compensation through the initially intended date of the agreement's termination, less by mutual consent.

- Should the congregation unilaterally terminate the agreement because of the Interim's demonstrated gross incompetence, or sexual/financial misconduct, having initiated all due process to remediate, counsel, correct, and restore the relationship, or because of the Interim's arrest due to criminal activity, the congregation compensates only for the actual time of service; more at the congregation's discretion.

Pastoral Covenants

The Interim Pastor agrees to the following covenant: *"Under no circumstances will I allow my name* to *be considered as a possible candidate for the settled position."* Likewise the church agrees that the Interim Pastor will not be considered as a possible candidate for the settled position.

Likewise, the Interim Pastor covenants to uphold the "_(name of denomination)_ Expectations of Interim Ministers."

In accepting this agreement, effective _(date)_, we hereby attach our signatures, making the covenant binding upon us in accordance with the above outlined terms, subject to the approval of the   governing board on _(date)_.

_____

Interim (Transitional) Pastor   *Date*

_____

Congregational Representative   *Date*

_____

Association/ Regional Representative   *Date*

Appendix B:
Survey Related to What's Broken in a Church

An important part of the transitional ministry process is identifying things in the church that would do well to be dealt with before the arrival of a settled pastor. One of the hardest jobs is getting churches to acknowledge what needs to change before the new pastor is on the field. It's never pleasant to look at what may be in need of fixing.

Ignoring things that aren't pleasant is a natural reaction. I've found it unproductive to ask a congregation, "What needs to change before a new pastor arrives?" The usual result is generalities about finances and attendance. Occasionally there will be some mention of things to do with by-laws.

As an interim, I'm often aware of things I could point out that need to change in the churches I serve. The problem is that these are things *I* could point out. The best chance for significant change comes when the *congregation* identifies the issues that need to be attended to. However, when I ask a direct question, people don't seem to give their answer much thought. They simply didn't want to acknowledge there are problems. It's out of this difficulty that I developed this survey.

I chose to use the word "broken" intentionally to put the focus on things that aren't working. There might still be denial, but at least the persons in denial have to engage with the idea that there might be something in need of change. I use the term for the shock value. It's turned out to be a good approach and useful data has come from the results.

Once the survey is given—mainly to church leaders and also made available to anyone in the church—the data is summarized and given to the transition team. We can use it to decide what issues should have priority in our efforts before a new settled pastor is on the scene.

If the expectation is that absolutely everything that needs to be attended to will be clearly identified, then that expectation is a little Pollyanna-ish. However, there's a lot that can be brought to the attention of the church. Even then, what comes to light will likely be more than can be addressed in a short period of time. The results may give helpful information to whoever is called to pastor a congregation.

This survey is more of a qualitative design than a quantitative design. A quantitative survey simply allows for answers to be counted and the assumption is the most answers are the most important issues. A quantitative design assumes there is a lot of information and some of the significant information may be identified by only a few people. Open-ended questions are used so anything can be brought out by those answering the survey. It would be possible to simply count how many people give similar answers to the questions, but that would defeat the purpose of this type of survey.

It requires much more effort to understand the meaning of the responses to a qualitative survey. The person or persons who are deciding how to interpret answers given on the survey should ask,

"What's behind the answer and what might have prompted the answers that were given?"

I start by listing the individual answers to each question. How many times a particular answer is given isn't important. Then I look for patterns in the answers. It is those patterns that are most important.

For example, in one survey it became obvious to me that behind many of the answers on different questions there was a sense of hopelessness. There was also a sense that someone would have to rescue the congregation. The expectation was that the incoming pastor would fix the things that were "broken" or that they could be fixed by having more people present. This, in effect, ameliorated the responsibility of the congregation.

In one of my reports, I pointed out that the congregation was waiting for someone else to fix things. I was also able to point out that there was no clear understanding of the actual mission of the church in its current time and place. These weren't things explicitly stated in the responses, but were issues that were hidden behind the responses. Needless to say, understanding this type of survey requires much more time and effort than understanding a quantitative survey.

This survey is given to the leadership of a congregation. That would be groups like the church council or church board as well as various teams of boards of the church. I make the assumption that these will be the people who have their fingers on the pulse of the congregation. That assumption may well be false. So, after emphasizing the importance of the leadership answering the survey, I offer it to everyone in the congregation. Since the number of responses don't count, there's no need to worry if someone answers it more than once.

I would recommend not giving the survey too soon after arriving as a transitional pastor. It's best if some time is given for trust to develop between the congregation and the person giving the survey.

A final word: This survey is a modified approach to quantitative measurement and it hasn't been peer reviewed. Despite that, I have found it very useful.

The actual survey follows. There's an introductory section and then the questions. I've laid it out as it would be presented to the congregation.

An Introduction to a Survey for This Time of Transition

The transition team is something that's new to some of our Baptist churches. In the past, when a pastor left, a search committee was selected to look for the pastor. All the attention was focused on calling a new pastor, and the church itself was overlooked. It's one thing to ask what we want to be different or the same in a new pastor. It is another question altogether to ask, "What needs to be new in the church before the pastor comes?" If this question isn't carefully and prayerfully considered, the pastor coming in may be forced down the same road as the previous pastor.

When calling a new pastor, a common question is, "What's the new pastor's vision for the church?" That's an impossible question. Anyone being interviewed won't have a clear understanding of what the church needs or what it's likely to do in the future. The church that will thrive under a new pastor must ask *itself* what needs to change in the church before a candidate is interviewed. It will make a big difference in who the church sees as a good candidate.

A transition team usually seeks to discover and make known what needs to change in a church. There are three questions that are central to the church's success:

Who are we?

Who is our neighbor?

What does God want us to do for our neighbor?

One way of approaching these questions is to ask, "What is broken in our church?" That's putting it in strong language that may put some people off. Another way of asking the same thing is to ask, "What isn't working well in this church?"

The attached survey is intended to get the congregation moving toward answers. These are open ended questions. The transition team will review the responses and decide what can be addressed in the time we have and what needs to be addressed under the leadership of a new pastor.

You don't have to sign this survey. If you do give us your name, we may reach out to you for clarification if there is something we are unclear about. If there's nothing unclear, this page will be discarded and disposed of.

Print name: _____

A Survey for
This Time of Transition

There are no right or wrong answers. This is asking you for your insight into this church and how it functions. Everyone is important to the final results. The space to answer is limited because we need to get to the heart of the matter. If you want to add additional pages, you may do so.

In general, what is broken about this church and in need of urgent repair?

_____

_____

_____

_____

_____

_____

What works well in this church?

_____

_____

_____

_____

_____

_____

What is broken about how this church is governed (by-laws)?

_____

_____

_____

_____

_____

_____

What is broken about the efficiency with which this church gets things done?

_____

_____

_____

_____

_____

_____

What is needed to make our church leaders more effective?

_____

_____

_____

_____

_____

How can selection of church leadership be made better?

_____

_____

_____

_____

_____

_____

_____

_____

How would you say the "spiritual health" of this church as a whole is?
Circle one for the overall general spiritual health of this church:

Spiritually very healthy

Spiritually more healthy than unhealthy

Neither healthy nor unhealthy

Leans toward being spiritually deficient

Spiritually, we are very unhealthy

Please add your comments about why you answered the way you did.

_____

_____

_____

_____

_____

What is needed, if anything, to increase this church's spiritual health?

_____

_____

_____

_____

_____

_____

What about how this church functions gets in the way of better spiritual health for all of the members?

_____

_____

_____

_____

_____

_____

What is this church's purpose for existing in this particular physical location?

_____

_____

_____

_____

_____

_____

What is unclear about why this church exists in this particular physical location?

_____

_____

_____

_____

_____

_____

What, if anything, is missing in this church's understanding of its mission in this community?

_____

_____

_____

_____

_____

225

What issues from the past are still causing problems for this church?

_____

_____

_____

_____

_____

_____

How does this church deal with conflicts that arise in the congregation?

_____

_____

_____

_____

_____

_____

How well does this church understand the community (within a ten-block radius) around us?

_____

_____

_____

_____

_____

_____

Is this church prepared for the future in this community? Please explain.

_____

_____

_____

_____

_____

_____

Is this church building in good physical shape? If not, what are the major things needed to get it in shape?

_____

_____

_____

_____

_____

_____

What about this church building will hinder new people from coming here?

_____

_____

_____

_____

_____

_____

How well are communications in this church handled? How could communication be improved?

Communications in this church are: (circle one)

Great   Okay   Neither great   Needs to be   Terrible
                 nor terrible   improved

Comments about communications in this church:

_____

_____

_____

_____

_____

How can communication in this church be improved?

_____

_____

_____

_____

_____

What is needed to increase the effectiveness of this church's social media presence?

_____

_____

_____

_____

_____

_____

How strong is this church's sense of hope for the future?

Very strong   Strong   So-so   Weak   There is no hope

_____

_____

_____

_____

_____

_____

What will enhance this church's hope for the future?

_____

_____

_____

_____

_____

_____

What stands in the way of this church being even more hopeful than it is?

_____

_____

_____

_____

_____

_____

How much do members of this church trust one another?

Circle one:

We trust each other without reservation

We have reservations about the motives of others

Trust depends on the persons involved

We are basically distrustful of one another

Very few, if any, in this church are really trustworthy

What is the reason for the trust or mistrust of one another?

_____

_____

_____

_____

_____

_____

_____

How effective is this church in supporting local mission efforts?

Effective   Somewhat effective   Ineffective

How effective is this church in supporting national mission efforts?

Effective   Somewhat effective   Ineffective

How effective is this church in supporting international mission efforts?

Effective   Somewhat effective   Ineffective

What can be done to increase our support of missions?

_____

_____

_____

_____

_____

_____

_____

Acknowledgements

I DON'T THINK I HAVE EVER written a book for which I didn't owe a debt of gratitude to a variety of people who either gave suggestions, put up with my crankiness, or who inspired my thinking as I was doing the writing. This book is no exception. In some ways, I have even more people to be indebted to for this work.

There have been several churches where I have worked as a Transitional Pastor. Some have had to put up with me as I learned and experimented with different ideas. I won't list them due to issues of confidentiality, but they are a part of this work.

I want to acknowledge the training I received through the Center for Congregational Health and the Interim Ministry Network. The leaders of the training events were great, and I appreciated their insight and approach to teaching.

I also want to thank Dr. Patricia Hernandez, an Associate General Secretary of the American Baptist Churches USA, who has transitional ministries as part of her job portfolio. She has always been supportive of the work I do. Our connection goes back for years before she took on responsibilities for the denomination and she has always been a supportive colleague and friend.

I also want to acknowledge the contribution of two men who took time to read the manuscript and make suggestions. The Reverend Edgar Owens and the Reverend Allan Martling. Ed is the consultant for transitional ministries of the American Baptist Churches of Michigan and leads a Ministerial Leadership Group for transitional pastors in the ABC-MI. Allan facilitates a support group for transitional minsters for the Michigan Conference of the United Church of Christ. I appreciate the suggestions they made and believe the final manuscript was much stronger for their input.

I would be remiss if I didn't acknowledge the contribution of my wife to all I do. There are times when I'm working on a manuscript that I'm not the easiest person to live with, and Carolyn has remained supportive in all my endeavors.

Finally, as with all my recent work, I want to acknowledge the special contribution of my editor, Erin McAuley. She has been of invaluable help in reading the manuscript and making suggestions for changes. She has also been a strength in checking for grammar and typographical errors as well as doing the cover design and layout of the book.

There are many other people who have supported me. I offer my most sincere thanks to each of you even if I am not listing names. If you find this work to be of value, you also owe a debt of gratitude to all these people.

Also by Ross T. Lucas

The ID Book: Unmasking the Soul and Revealing
Your True Mission in Life

Available in both print and e-book from *www.lulu.com*

Print: https://bit.ly/theidbook
E-book: https://bit.ly/theidebook

Or from your favorite online retailer.

About the Author

ROSS T. LUCAS attended undergraduate studies at Indiana State University in Terre Haute, Indiana, with a major in History and a minor in Philosophy. He earned a Master of Divinity from Southern Baptist Theological Seminary in Louisville, Kentucky, a M.S. in Counseling and Guidance from Southwestern Oklahoma State University in Weatherford, Oklahoma, and a Ph.D. in Educational Psychology from Indiana University in Bloomington, Indiana.

Ross has served on numerous community, church, and professional committees; including having been chairman for the midwest region of the American Association of Pastoral Counselors, center director for the Windsor/Detroit community of the ManKind Project, president of the ABC Ministers Council of Michigan, president of the Chaplains and Pastoral Counselors' Ministers Council of the American Baptist Churches USA, and having served on the region board of the American Baptist Churches of Michigan. He is currently involved in transitional ministries, having worked with churches in Michigan and New York.

Ross enjoys painting, writing poems and short stories, and his photographs have been displayed in several juried exhibitions. He is an Eagle Scout and holds a first degree Black Belt in Judo.

Made in the USA
Columbia, SC
09 July 2024

38364261R00152